Cambridge Elements ≡

Elements of Sustainability: Science, Policy, Practice
edited by
Editor-in-Chief
Arun Agrawal
University of Michigan

GIRL POWER

Sustainability, Empowerment, and Justice

Jin In
Boston University

CAMBRIDGE
UNIVERSITY PRESS

Shaftesbury Road, Cambridge CB2 8EA, United Kingdom

One Liberty Plaza, 20th Floor, New York, NY 10006, USA

477 Williamstown Road, Port Melbourne, VIC 3207, Australia

314–321, 3rd Floor, Plot 3, Splendor Forum, Jasola District Centre, New Delhi – 110025, India

103 Penang Road, #05–06/07, Visioncrest Commercial, Singapore 238467

Cambridge University Press is part of Cambridge University Press & Assessment, a department of the University of Cambridge.

We share the University's mission to contribute to society through the pursuit of education, learning and research at the highest international levels of excellence.

www.cambridge.org
Information on this title: www.cambridge.org/9781009481885

DOI: 10.1017/9781009481922

First published 2024

A catalogue record for this publication is available from the British Library.

ISBN 978-1-009-48188-5 Hardback
ISBN 978-1-009-48191-5 Paperback
ISSN 2635-0211 (online)
ISSN 2635-0203 (print)

Girl Power

Sustainability, Empowerment, and Justice

Elements of Sustainability: Science, Policy, Practice

DOI: 10.1017/9781009481922
First published online: September 2024

Jin In
Boston University
Author for correspondence: Jin In, jin@4ggl.org

Abstract: Power. Gender. Sustainability. This Element harnesses powerful new data about gender and sustainability, presents inspiring stories of empowerment, and introduces a framework for building empowerment muscles. First, from a pioneering global survey, it unveils three shocking truths about young women's empowerment. It also compiles significant data on systemic gender disempowerment intersecting environmental degradation, violence, and exclusion, as well as profound societal impact if girls and women were fully empowered. Second, from climate activist Greta Thunberg to the all-girl Afghan robotics team, the #NeverAgain movement against gun violence, and the Hong Kong pro-democracy movement, today's empowered girls are a transformative force for change. Each modeling a distinct skill – an empowerment muscle – seven case studies present empowerment muscles of focus, solidarity, hope, courage, advocacy, endurance, and healing. Third, unlike most works using empowerment nebulously, this Element concretizes empowerment – a set of muscles each reader can build and strengthen through "workout" training exercises.

Keywords: empowerment, sustainability, equity, gender equality, justice

ISBNs: 9781009481885 (HB), 9781009481915 (PB), 9781009481922 (OC)
ISSNs: 2635-0211 (online), 2635-0203 (print)

Contents

Dedication

A wise person once noted that full sight requires hindsight, foresight, and insight. This Element is dedicated to those who have gifted me these sights — foremost, my life's mentor Barbara Crocker, today's and tomorrow's Girl Power.

Acknowledgements

I am deeply grateful for the young women who have helped on *Girl Power*, especially Gabriela Cordero, Natalie Kimber, Charlotte Fleming, Noelle Cohn, and Amy Thomas. I am also indebted to Professor Benjamin Sovacool and my dear friend Dylan Furszyfer Del Rio for their unwavering support and cheerleading.

There is no tool for development more effective than the empowerment of women.
—Kofi Annan, 7th UN Secretary General

Empowering women is key to building a future we want.
—Amartya Sen, Nobel Prize Laureate in Economics

Let us tell the world and let us tell it with pride:
The empowerment of women is the empowerment of all humanity!
—Boutros Boutros-Ghali, 6th UN Secretary General

Preface: Girls and Power

Have you ever thought about the word *girl*? What are some initial thoughts that come to your mind?

Today, the word *girl* has a demeaning or ridiculing connotation. It is intentionally used to depict or bully boys as being sissy, weak, cowardly, inferior in strength and character – in sum, not masculine. Furthermore, phrases like "throw like a girl" or "run like a girl" are said about them to humiliate or shame their athletic ability. Even when the word is used to describe females, it's to hyper-feminize, perpetuating the gender stereotype with over-the-top pink, curlicues, glitter or sparkles, not being serious, or simply being a "bimbo."

Now, juxtapose the word *girl* with *power*. Just saying *power* gives you a boost of energy as it depicts strength, confidence, and dynamism. In Western, capitalistic societies, it is associated with people with prominent wealth, position, and prestige. Headlines like "world's most powerful people" and "world's most powerful women" are used to captivate and hold our attention as we adore those named powerful.

Thus, it may seem audacious to use the two words together – *Girl Power* – depicting the demographic group that is seen and treated as the weakest as the most powerful, in reality. However, this wasn't always a dichotomy. The word *girl* began as a gender-neutral word. Yes, it was used for both girls *and* boys. A frequently cited example is *The Canterbury Tales* in 1387. The great poet Geoffrey Chaucer wrote:[1]

In daunger hadde he at his owene gyse
The yonge gerles of the diocise,
And knew hir conseil, and was al hir reed.

Here, it's the secrets of young people, not just "gerles."

Unfortunately, *girl* was gendered after the 1400s, and when the word is used together with *power* in the modern era, even with good intentions, it generally perpetuates gender stereotypes, especially when they are used with old thinking and an outdated mindset. For example, a program called Girl Power was created in 1997 as a national public education campaign to galvanize parents, schools, communities, religious organizations, health care providers, and other caring adults to make sustained efforts to reinforce the self-confidence of girls ages nine to fourteen. Created in the Office of the Secretary, US Department of Health and Human Services, with both public and private partners, it had tremendous potential.

Unfortunately, it was dumbed down. Cartoonish female figurines dressed in pink were portrayed mimicking activities boys do, mainly sports. Perpetuating the gender stereotype that only boys are strong and powerful, it was as if the program encouraged caretakers to turn girls into boys.

Words and their meanings evolve – forward as well as backward – at the rate of our consciousness and mindset. Thus, it's essential to be vigilant, critically examining or seeking experiences in a new light. And in this case, what if we view the word *girl* simply as is, without the stereotypes?

This is how I learned and associated with the word. Immigrating to the United States at age eight, and learning English as a second language, *girl* was my identifier, my affinity group. And the words together, *Girl Power*, describe my empowerment journey – building my internal strength and resilience through community service and social justice action. Later in life, pursuing a professional career specializing in Girl Power, I witnessed the same with girls around the world taking action to make their world better. Like me, this pathway built their agency and capacity – internal power or empowerment.

Now, what about the word *power*?

Power is the strength required to bring about social, political, and economic change.
Power without love is reckless . . .
Power at its best is love implementing the demands of justice, and justice at its best is
power correcting everything that stands against love.
—Martin Luther King, Jr.[2]

Power in and of itself isn't bad. It's simply energy, a resource. One form of resource that is exchangeable is money. What we may not recognize is that money is currency, and like current or water, it is meant to flow – from one person to another. In fact, the moment it's stagnant or hoarded in one place, it becomes toxic.

This is why the imbalance of power – hoarding, dominating, and abusing it – is at the root of all injustices, inequities, and social illnesses. Furthermore, no matter the crisis – climate degradation, poverty, corruption, violence, and war – the ones without power are impacted the most. As the sayings go: "Poverty is sexist," and "climate change is sexist."

Now, think about the words *gender* and *empowerment*. What do they mean? Box 1 offers some varying definitions.

So, how should we transform our thinking and use of power – energy? The law of conservation of energy states that energy can be neither created nor destroyed. It can only be converted from one form to another – transformed power. This is empowerment, and this Element is about that transformed power,

---

BOX 1 CONCEPTUALIZING "GENDER" AND "EMPOWERMENT"

The terms "gender" and "empowerment" appear often in news stories or speeches, but what do they actually mean?

Gender is often associated with sex, one's biological identity as male or female, but such a conception has changed over the past century. Before the 1960s, gender meant family, whether one was masculine or feminine. But since then, it has evolved to also refer to particular personality traits and behaviors associated with women or men, such as men being violent or aggressive, or women passive and caring. Gender can also include differences between social groups of "men" and "women" that are the product of unequal relationships, meaning gender can be conceived as a hierarchy of exclusion in society, where some genders (men) may have more privilege or power than other groups (women). Gender can lastly be thought of as performative, as something an individual does and repro-duces through their own identity, their practices, and their social inter-actions with others.

Empowerment also has multiple meanings, and it can include the authority or power given to somebody to do something they want to do, or the process of enhancing one's own ability to be stronger, more confi-dent, or more control of their life. One definition offered by Page and Czuba sees empowerment as "a multi-dimensional social process that helps people gain control over their own lives. It is a process that fosters power in people for use in their own lives, their communities and in their society, by acting on issues they define as important."[3] Surveys of practi-tioners around the world have identified six mechanisms of empowerment (knowledge; agency; opportunity; capacity-building; resources; and sus-tainability), five domains of empowerment (health; economic; political; resource; and spiritual), and three levels (individual; community; and organizational).

Source: Drawn from [4,5]

which is bringing about impactful social and political changes around the world. Girl Power is not only transformed power; it is, in fact, the power our world needs – right now.

With this said, my hope is that you – the reader – think about how you too can be a part of Girl Power. Our world is a mess, and we need every single person to become an agent of change. To begin, what do you see as the most important issue in your world, now? What are the skills – empowerment muscles – needed to take action? What is the first step toward this action?

Let's get to work and build our muscles of empowerment!

1 Introduction: The Status of Today's Girls

This Element is about *power*. More specifically, it's about an emerging power that is awakening and transforming our world today: *Girl Power*.

To begin, achieving Girl Power is extraordinary. To show just how difficult it is, let's begin with a basic question: Are there more *males* or *females* on the planet, today? Surprisingly, most people answer this incorrectly. In fact, even world leaders, experts in global development, and women's rights activists are misinformed, using assumptions and ironically perpetuating a myth that does not address the mindset that is at the root of gender inequality.

The correct answer is males. Yes, *males*. And with sixty-seven million extra males, globally, in 2017, our planet was the most gender – and power – imbalanced than in any other time in recorded history.[6] Figure 1 shows the

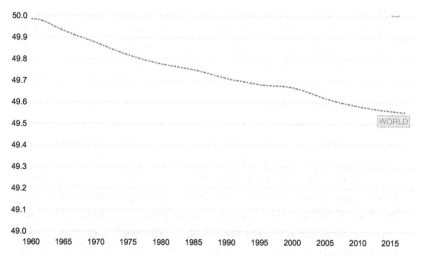

Figure 1 Global female population as a percentage of the total, 1960–2017.
Source: World Bank, used under a CC BY-4.0 license.

World Bank's sex disaggregated data of the world population from 1960 to 2017. Based on it, if we created a brand-new country with just the extra males – sixty-seven million – it would be the twenty-first most populous country, larger than France.

How did we get here? How did we create such a gender-imbalanced world with gender disparity increasing, not decreasing, in the modern era?

If left to Mother Nature, she would balance the sexes, naturally.[5] Instead, we have created a man-made, male-majority world with powerful technologies that scale and amplify our primitive mindset – that males are more valuable than females.

In fact, today, all three of these realities exist simultaneously:

- An antiquated mindset that still justifies stoning a girl to death for being raped by a man as "honor."
- Outdated institutions that are deeply engrained with systemic and systematic gender discrimination.
- Hubristic technology that allows sex-selective abortion on a mass scale.

The United Nations reported that 5,000 females are killed annually in the name of honor.[8] Human rights advocates outcry that this number is too low, as honor killing is vastly underreported.[9] Another sex-selective method of killing is abortion. India alone kills 2,000 girl babies in the womb every day.[10] According to data from James Madison University:[11]

- There are 140 males for every 100 females in India and China, compared to the global ration of 105 boys for every 100 girls;
- 1 [in] 4 girls die before puberty in these regions;
- 200 million women are missing each year because of gendercide;
- 100,000 female adults are murdered each year from dowry violence – harassment by husbands and in-laws in an effort to extort an increased dowry;
- 14 million forced abortions are done a year, up to the 9th month of pregnancy in China;
- 500 women a day commit suicide in China.

Our world wages a chronic, systemic, and practically invisible war against girls. Two countries alone have exacerbated this crisis on a continental scale. China and India combined have 80 million extra males.[12] In India, one in sixteen babies is killed in sex-selective abortion. China has the greatest imbalance of reported sex ratios on record, with a gender imbalance of 122 percent for those aged zero to four in favor of boys, as Table 1 indicates.

However, looking superficially at the raw numbers does not tell the whole story. Digging deeper and carefully reviewing the ratio unveils another story – regional

Table 1 Reported sex ratios at birth and sex ratios of the population aged zero to four in China, 1953–2005 (boys per 100 girls)

Year	Sex ratio at birth	Sex ratio, age 0–4
1953	–	107.0
1964	–	105.7
1982	108.5	107.1
1990	111.4	110.2
1995	115.6	118.4
1999	117.0	119.5
2005	118.9	122.7

trends where a deep-seated mindset penetrates and permeates with regard to gender and power. Case in point: Although in raw numbers, China and India are by far the worst offenders of "gendercide," proportionally, males make up 51.3 percent of China's population and 52 percent of India's.[13] Compare this to the Middle East: Bahrain's 63.7 percent males, Oman's 66 percent males, United Arab Emirates' 69.4 percent males, and the worst, Qatar's 75.5 percent males. This illuminates a mindset that permeates the region – one that has given value, preferential treatment, and *power* to males. The Middle East is also the most conflict-ridden region.

Indeed, in many cultures, the three deadliest words are "it's a girl." Just imagine if the DNA of your eyes or hair color could get you killed. And yet, this is exactly what we allow and are complicit in – the killing of baby girls around the world. That is, having XX chromosomes is a death sentence. More than 100 million baby girls have been killed, forcibly aborted, and left to die simply because of this chromosome, something the *Economist* termed gendercide as they put this alarming statistic on their cover in March 2010 (see Figure 2).[14] One hundred forty-two million females are "missing" today who should be alive.[15] By 2035, 150 million females will be missing.[16] One way to see the magnitude of this injustice is that more baby girls have been killed, aborted, or neglected and left to die than the total killed from all wars in the twentieth century. Another way is that more baby girls have been killed, aborted, or neglected and left to die than the total killed from all genocides of the twentieth century. The top five genocides by total death include the Soviet famine (10 million deaths), the Holocaust (6 million), Cambodia (2 million), Armenia (1 million). Rwanda, Bosnia, and Darfur together involved 1.2 million deaths.

This isn't just a birth problem. Even if a baby girl has the chance to live, she faces a steep uphill battle at every stage of her life. Below are obstacles a girl faces just through adolescence:

Figure 2 Documenting gendercide and 100 million missing girls in the media.
Source: *The Economist*, used with permission.

- Every two seconds, a girl is forced to marry.[17]
- One out of every five girls becomes a mother before her eighteenth birthday, and for girls ages fifteen to nineteen, pregnancy and childbirth complications are leading killers, globally.[18]
- One out of every ten girls is raped or forced into a sexual act, and even in the United States, ages twelve to thirty-four are when girls are at the highest risk of being raped or sexually assaulted.[19]
- Every eleven minutes, a girl dies from a violent act.[20]

Facing just one of these horrendous sufferings is traumatizing enough. And yet, many girls experience multiple. That is, a girl who is forced to marry as a child is more likely to face domestic violence, sexual assault, rape, and death during childbirth.[21] Furthermore, this is only the beginning, as an endless list of possible violent acts awaits her throughout her life: female genital cutting, honor killing, sex slavery, rape as a weapon of war, and many more. A degrading cultural practice called *jaboya* exists across sub-Saharan Africa where fishing is a significant income source. Female fishers – making up 80 percent of the workers – trade sex for fish, literally, in an effort to secure a financially sufficient lifestyle. Furthermore, girls will offer "sex for fish" to male fishers, even at the expense of being infected with HIV and other sexually transmitted infections.[22]

Femicide, the most severe form of gender-based violence, still occurs, and in some countries, such as South Africa, more than 2,400 women are killed each year simply because of their gender.[23] Globally, although data are often incomplete, we know that at least 89,000 women were killed intentionally in 2022, of whom 48,800 were killed by an intimate partner or a family member.[24]

Each and every violent act degrades the human soul. And yet, this is exactly what societies allow – the stripping away of dignity and power – to girls and women. Indeed, every single act of violence is about *power* – power and control over another human being. Although the symptoms look different depending on the locality – that is, teen pregnancy in some countries, child marriage in other countries – the disease is the same: the patriarchal power structure, which does not value females.

The moral arc of gender justice is long, but it has been paved by our foremothers. In the United States, from Susan B. Anthony and Elizabeth Cady Stanton to Sojourner Truth, Harriet Tubman, and many more, women before us relentlessly fought for women's rights, voices, and freedom. The platinum jubilee of their hard work was recognized in 2020: the hundredth anniversary of the Nineteenth Amendment, women's right to vote.

As the world rallies to combat the climate crisis, poverty, conflict, and war, as well as to promote social progress and sustainable development, we must focus on and target the group with the most body of evidence for impact. Today, we know who they are and what we need to do – empower adolescent girls and young women.

More than one billion girls and young women are poised to be the next generation of innovators, scientists, entrepreneurs, political leaders, and humanitarians who will change the world. This largest cohort in history is breaking barriers and glass ceilings, defying stereotypes, and working to abolish outdated traditions. Foremost, they are using their voices to initiate, advocate for, and lead global movements for social and political change.

This is *Girl Power*. From climate activist Greta Thunberg to an all-girl Afghan robotics team and the ninja warriors at the frontline of the Hong Kong protest fighting one of the most powerful governments, China – girls are real-life superheroes, protecting the planet and seeking justice for all. Each story in this Element profiles a superhero or a superhero group, demonstrating a superpower – a muscle of empowerment.

To preview, one superhero is climate activist and TIME Person of the Year, Greta Thunberg. Her superpower – empowerment muscle – is *focus*. Despite being bullied for being autistic, she uses and channels the exact trait that autism gifts her – the ability to focus intensely – into powerful action, sparking global awareness and movement.

Another superhero is Fatemah. Her superpower is *hope*. Despite facing the traumatic killing/murder of her father by the Taliban, on top of living in a patriarchal society with entrenched gender discrimination, Fatemah somehow practices hope by pursuing education in STEM: science, technology, engineering, math. What gives her hope is inspiring hope in other girls just like her in Afghanistan. Through herstory, we will learn how hope can change not just a community or country but also the world.

Many of us may not know the unwaveringly unified citizens of Hong Kong, particularly the adolescent girls and young women. At the frontline of the protests, serving as a human shield against the almighty military force of China, these ferocious ninja warriors were practicing the wisdom of the great spiritual leader Hillel: *If not now, when? If not me, who?* In so doing, they are demonstrating what may be the most important empowerment muscle – solidarity. Solidarity evokes people power and collective change.

Lastly, *Girl Power* includes my own herstory and journey of empowerment. It began in one of the poorest countries on the planet. And yet, unlike most girls living in the developing world, I witnessed my birth country, South Korea, develop economically, skyrocketing in GDP in one generation – my generation. It went from one of the poorest world economies to the eleventh largest.

However, money does not buy empowerment – nor gender equality. On the contrary, the global data I collected on young women's empowerment showed that those living in rich countries are not more empowered than those in poor countries. In fact, it may be the opposite. Young women in poor countries face more obstacles and hardships, and overcoming them trains them to build their empowerment muscles and resilience – developing their inner power, agency, and capacity.

Thus, *Girl Power* is also a *how-to* Element – how to build our own muscles of empowerment. Guided by training exercises at the end of each herstory, along with the first-ever data on young women's empowerment collected on a global level, this Element will concretize empowerment, showing what empowerment is, *exactly* – not some nebulous idea or wishful thinking but, in fact, the process and training of concrete muscles that we all can build, strengthen, and use to take action in our crisis-filled world.

Girl Power is a gamechanger. It is an underappreciated intellectual, social, political, and emotional resource throughout the world. Moreover, girls often have the most direct experience with environmental challenges. Girls labor in hot, unventilated homes with outdated cookstoves. Girls collect water in large plastic jugs from a communal water source far from their homes. Girls gather sticks or coal pieces to burn to keep the family warm at night. Girls are shuttled to and from school and activities in gas guzzling cars. Girls are interested in the science that would solve many of these issues. In this way, as this Element will show, Girl Power may just be our future's most powerful force for change.

As you may see already, this is no ordinary academic Element. To show and amplify Girl Power, it seeks to inform and galvanize a diverse array of audiences. First and foremost are young adults, especially adolescent girls and young women, studying science in schools and universities. Second are policymakers and planners developing policies and programs with civil society groups at local, national, and international levels. This includes multilateral organizations like UN Women and the World Bank or the Asian Development Bank. Third is scholars of sustainability, including early career (male and female) researchers who may not see the connections between their work and gender empowerment. Last but not least, the public as a whole must transform its mindset about girls. Furthermore, we can all learn from Girl Power – a general audience of ordinary people who can build and use the muscles of empowerment to do extraordinary things to make the world better for all.

2 Data: The Gender–Justice–Sustainable Development Nexus

Although various metrics of gender equity and equality exist, perhaps the most well known is the gender gap, which measures systematic differences in the outcomes that men and women achieve in the labor market or society.[25] The World Economic Forum benchmarks the global gender gap across the four core dimensions of economic participation and opportunity, education, health and survival, and political empowerment. The longest-standing indexed gender tracker, the Global Gender Gap Report, estimates that at the current rate in 2023, it will take an additional 131 years for our world to reach gender parity.[26] For some particular regions, such as East Asia and the Pacific, it may even take until the twenty-second century (see Figure 3). Although the exact number of years to parity may change slightly from year to year, the fact that it will take at least one century for gender parity to be our reality is unacceptable. The United Nations warns that less than 1 percent of women and girls live in countries with high women's empowerment.[27] Conversely, more than 90 percent of the world's female population – 3.1 billion women and girls – live in countries characterized by low or middle women's empowerment and low or middle performance in achieving gender parity. In simpler terms, women globally achieve only 60 percent of their full potential.

With all this said and shown with significant data, what if we just don't care? We don't care about achieving gender parity, nor about girls. Does gender imbalance have negative consequences on societies?

From economy to mental health and well-being, public safety, and even national security, the current gross gender imbalance with a massive number

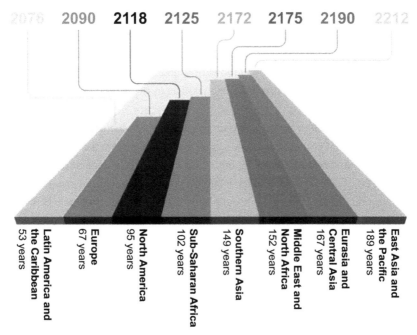

2076 **2090** **2118** **2125** 2172 **2175** **2190** 2212

Latin America and
the Caribbean
53 years

Europe
67 years

North America
95 years

Sub-Saharan Africa
102 years

Southern Asia
149 years

Middle East and
North Africa
152 years

Eurasia and
Central Asia
167 years

East Asia and
the Pacific
189 years

Figure 3 When different global regions will close their gender gap.
Source: [26]

of extra males has a devastating impact. More importantly, women's empowerment – particularly empowered girls – has demonstrated a transformative impact on families, communities, and society as a whole. Based on a thematic analysis of the academic and policy literature, this section identifies seven different dimensions of sustainability writ large – climate change, natural resource extraction via forestry and fishing, energy access, water use, education, health, and national security – and shows how they all impact girls deeply and directly. It also shows how girls can deeply and directly impact these areas of sustainability as well.

2.1 Girls and Climate Change

Our planet is no longer warming. It is downright boiling. From wildfires, severe air quality alerts, and record-breaking temperatures to extreme weather disasters like tornadoes, hurricanes, and flooding becoming more intense and the norm, we are now facing a "new abnormal."

Indeed, the climate is changing, rapidly. And yet, human beings are not. While some of us are still debating and denying climate change, even those who know the gravity of global warming and are actively working on solutions, most are just focusing on developing new technologies – more stuff.

Just as we can't bomb our way out of wars, we can't "make more stuff" our way out of the climate crisis. For true sustainability, first, we must protect the most vulnerable, the ones who are impacted the most by weather disasters. Second, we must focus on – empowering and supporting – the groups that would have the greatest impact in societies. The most "bang for the buck," as the saying goes.

The first: Climate change is sexist! Yes, the most vulnerable, and those who bear the brunt of climate devastation, are women and girls in the most marginalized communities. Just like every other humanitarian challenge of our time, the climate crisis also perpetuates and magnifies systemic inequalities and inequities, and the imbalance of power. For example, extreme heat costs everyone. However, the economic loss is overwhelmingly greater for women than men: 260 percent versus 76 percent, respectively.[28] This is mostly due to unpaid domestic work, like childcare and other caregiving, compounded by the existing unequal pay. In totality, the economic consequence of just three countries – India, Nigeria, and the United States – alone is at least $120 billion.[28]

Another sexist practice compounding the devastation of climate change is land-ownership and agriculture. According to the International Labor Organization, women are essential to agriculture, contributing 41 percent of the agricultural labor force, globally, and even more in low-income countries, nearly 50 percent.[29] And yet, females are not the owners of the land that they harvest and cultivate. It has been estimated that only 20 percent of the world's land is female owned, although the United Nations Food and Agriculture Organization reports half of that – as low as 10 percent.[30] This is due to the fundamental fact that worldwide, females do not have equal, or any, rights to own land. Also, they don't have access to agricultural resources and services. Furthermore, they are excluded from decision-making processes in agriculture, as well as climate resilient policy development. The exclusion isn't just in agriculture. They are also excluded in fishery and forestry.

The irony and the profound reality is that empowering the most vulnerable group – women and girls in the most marginalized communities – is in fact the most powerful, transformative, and sustainable solution to combating climate change. For example, one estimate shows that if all female farmers were empowered and had equal access to resources, their agricultural production would increase by 20–30 percent, 100–150 million people could be fed, and foremost, the planet could reduce carbon dioxide emissions by 2.1 gigatons by 2050.[31] Again, simply by empowering all female farmers, we can: feed 100–150 million people, increase farming production by 20–30 percent, and reduce carbon dioxide emissions by 2.1 gigatons by 2050. The Food and Agriculture Organization of the United Nations also noted that if African smallholder female farmers had more equal access to land, labor, information, technology, fertilizer, and water, then agricultural production across the continent would increase by 20 percent.[32] As philanthropist Melinda Gates noted when reading about these trends, "people are going hungry while we try to figure out how to address gender inequality and empower women."[33]

Women's empowerment is powerful in agriculture – as well as in forestry and fishery (which are explored in greater detail in Section 2.2). Furthermore, it is important to give women and girls the power and agency for them to build climate resilient communities, including policy development and decision-making. Indeed, it has been shown that female parliamentarians at the national level adopt more stringent climate change policies.[34] This results in lower carbon emissions across the nation. The inclusion of women leads to more equitable planning and public participation in the design of cities, as well as cities with more livable and green public spaces, cities that are more walkable, cities that have more affordable housing, cities with better physical and emotional well-being, and cities that are generally more sustainable.[35]

Indeed, Project Drawdown, an extensive group of climate researchers, scientists, business leaders, and policymakers, has declared that empowering girls – educating girls and family planning – is one of the most effective and long-lasting tools to stop greenhouse gases in the atmosphere *and* reduce them (see Figure 4).[36] For example, a nation's climate resilience can improve (on average) by 3.2 points for every additional year a girl stays in school.[37]

2.2 Girls and Natural Resource Extraction

Unlike most sectors in environmental sustainability, forestry gives access to ownership and management of land and thereby gives people in this field a built-in personal growth process – empowerment. This is noted in the interviews conducted with female woodland owners in Western Oregon.[38] Additionally, these female foresters belong to a special community group, Women Owning Woodlands network (WOWnet) – a horizontal, small group with a praxis-based approach; the added benefit of belonging to this group multiplied their sense of agency and control.

With this said, female foresters are not immune to systemic discrimination and the social challenges females face in their societies. This is noted in the Sundarbans mangrove forest program. A UNESCO World Heritage site, the Sundarbans mangrove forest lies on the Bay of Bengal and is one of the largest such forests in the world. Thus, women's participation in the resource management and conservation of this majestic forest would be impactful. And yet, due to the cultural constraints girls and women face, dictated by the patriarchal social system, female representation in participation is low.[39]

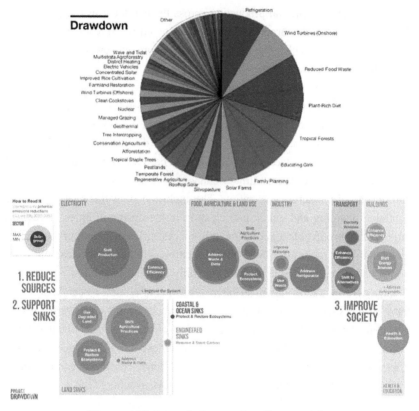

Figure 4 Eighty solutions to the climate crisis.

Source: Project Drawdown. Project Drawdown created climate and financial models for eighty solutions to climate change. The researchers found that if the world implements the initial eighty solutions over a thirty-year period using a "reasonable yet optimistic forecast," the total amount of CO_2 avoided and sequestered amounts to 1,051 gigatons by 2050. To achieve "drawdown," or the point where greenhouse gases in the atmosphere begin to decline, we'd need to ramp them up a bit more, particularly renewable energy, to get to 1,442 gigatons by 2050.

Now, going from local to global, a program funded and conducted by the International Fund for Agricultural Development (IFAD) focuses on gender equality and women's empowerment as it recognizes that women can become a powerful force in transforming the lives of their families and communities. Through their global partnership program on non-timber forest products (NTFP), IFAD collected knowledge on how to encourage broader and more significant support for rural women in the NTFP sector and to adopt measures that enable both women and men to benefit equally from its development.[40] Furthermore, they highlighted supporting women, multidimensionally – in division of labor, access to credit and market information, environmental issues, and so on. All of this begins with seeing females as agents of powerful change.[40]

Girls and women are also leading the way for promoting more sustainable fishing practices, particularly those that do not exploit human beings, sexually. Case in point, campaigns collectively known as "No Sex for Fish" are being created across sub-Saharan African communities. The programs give female fish traders access to boats and other fishing resources, thereby empowering them with the tools to fish themselves rather than needing to trade sex in order to eat.[41] This has been shown to improve food and economic securities, as well as empower women. Indeed, giving women in India more control in fishing practices has been shown to improve social, economic, legal, and political parameters – all at the same time. It expanded access to fish vending, fish drying, prawn peeling, sorting, grading, fish packing, and net making. Likewise, a program in Kenya gave women access to their own boats, avoiding those who sought to exploit them, sexually or otherwise.[42,43] An intervention in Uganda, the NutriFish project, has had a positive impact on fishing communities as well as empowering women fishers by giving them decision-making power over their incomes and increased access to credit to start small businesses through saving groups. In sum, giving women tools and control of their fishing practices led to decreasing and diminishing an exploitive cultural practice.

2.3 Girls and Energy Access

In many cultures, girls and women are the primary collectors of fuelwood for cooking, the primary cooks, the primary energy users, and, when old enough, the primary childminders, placing themselves and those they care for at a higher risk of exposure to biomass smoke and negative health consequences.[44] For instance, women comprise the majority of those vulnerable to energy scarcity; time spent in fuel collection can range from one to five hours per day, frequently with an infant strapped to a woman's back. As the Asian Development Bank has reported, "the energy–poverty nexus has a distinct gender bias: of the world's poor, 70 percent are women."[45] Figure 5 shows how the health impacts of traditional fuel use have a significant gender bias,[46] and just how hazardous it is to young women and children.[47] Indeed, the global burden of disease study published by the *Lancet* estimates that four million people die prematurely each year from indoor air pollution from this traditional cooking, an amount greater than deaths from malaria, HIV/AIDS, or tuberculosis.[48] Most of these deaths are women and young children.[49]

This isn't just about health – or more accurately, about illness. It is also about *equity*. As Figure 6 illustrates, over the course of a typical year in Tanzania,

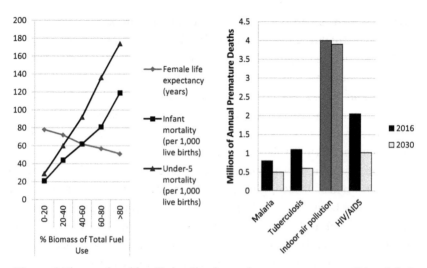

Figure 5 The gendered health implications of energy poverty, traditional fuel use, and avoidable premature deaths.

Source: [47]

a man will spend about 500 hours with chores, fuel collection, cooking, and other tasks compared to almost 2,000 hours – four times that of a man – for a woman. This woman will also carry almost ninety tons of fuelwood or other loads, whereas a man will carry less than twelve tons.[50] Figure 6 also shows the long distance most women travel in Tanzania to collect wood, with some in Singida traveling more than ten kilometers (6.2 miles) every single day. And for those living in countries with harsh winter climates, women gather firewood twice a day during warmer summer months to stockpile wood for the winter.

Indeed, the irony is that those with less physical strength in general – females – are doing the heavy lifting, literally. In fact, in some developing countries, the group with the least amount of physical strength, girls, spend the most time collecting wood and water – 3.5 times more than boys of the same age and a shocking seven times more than adult males.[51] All this adds up to an extraordinary amount of time. In India, for instance, a woman spends forty hours per month just collecting fuel, and many walk long distances – more than six kilometers (3.7 miles) round trip.[50] This totals a whopping thirty billion hours annually – eighty-two million hours every day – that girls and women in India spend collecting fuelwood, with an economic burden (including time invested and illnesses) of $6.7 billion (300 billion rupees) per year.[52] Across Africa, a woman has to carry twenty kilograms (forty-four pounds) of fuelwood a distance of five kilometers (3.1 miles) every day.[53]

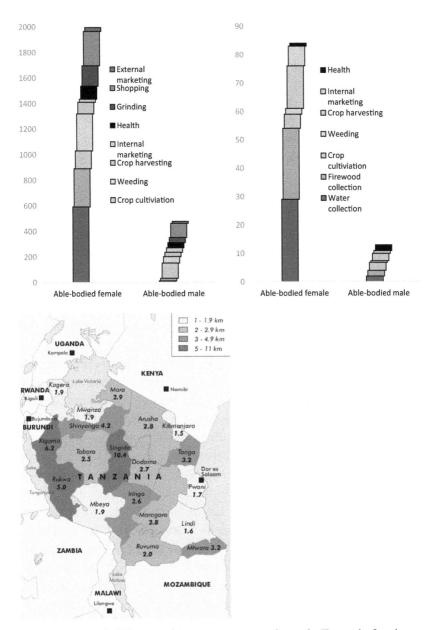

Figure 6 Annual differences between women and men in Tanzania for chores (in hours, top left image) and hauling items (in tons, top right image) as well as distances traveled (in kilometers, bottom image) per day.

Source: [28]

Additionally, current energy production entails occupational hazards that almost uniquely affect women and children. This is because when females carry heavy weights – of forty to fifty kilograms, or about as much as their own body weight – they suffer frequent falls, back aches, bone fractures, eye problems, headaches, rheumatism, anemia, and even miscarriages.[52] The energy needs of rural women can be further marginalized if men control community forests, plantations, or woodlots, and if there are other "high value" wood demands on the community that displace their foraging grounds for fuel.

Conflict and war compound this challenge for girls and women: physical and sexual violence on top of energy poverty. For example, hundreds of Somali refugee women were raped while gathering fuelwood around camps bordering the Somali–Kenyan border, and women in Sarajevo, Bosnia, faced sniper fire while gathering fuel.[53] In Darfur, Sudan, women were frequently assaulted and attacked while collecting fuelwood; many trekked hours at dusk and dawn to avoid the hot sun, and yet, these are the most dangerous times to walk alone.[53] In India, brides have committed suicide simply because they couldn't meet their family's fuel needs.[53]

Therefore, women and children are "the prime beneficiaries of rural electrification."[54] The availability of modern energy means women save time – from collecting water and wood to any other old-time source of energy modernity has resolved. Moreover, modern energy reduces risks – from injuries, as well as assault and rape, particularly in conflict and war zones. Women with electricity in their homes are better able to balance paid work and household chores, and may even have more time for leisure than women without electricity, helping to leverage a woman's status both inside and outside of the household.[55] A global study found that "reduced drudgery for women and increased access to nonpolluting power for lighting, cooking, and other household and productive purposes can have dramatic effects on women's levels of education, literacy, nutrition, health, economic opportunities and involvement in community activities."[56] It also concluded that electrification would require much less time for performing basic subsistence activities (i.e. water pumping and grain grinding) and can power labor saving and income-generating equipment. Small-scale manufacturing, food processing industries, trading, and marketing opportunities are all greatly expanded when energy services are available to girls and women, having direct positive influences on them and their communities.

Furthermore, reliable energy services offer opportunities for women's enterprises and agricultural processing to develop. Energy for mechanical agricultural processing equipment can reduce the daily effort of women's manual labor.

One study documented a correlation between modern energy access and small-scale enterprises operated by women, including beer brewing, rice parboiling, tortilla making, baking, shea butter production, palm oil processing, pottery making, hotels, and restaurants.[57] In Bangladesh, Grameen Shakti has established forty-five Grameen Technology Centers that have trained more than 176,000 heads of households (mostly women) in the proper use and maintenance of solar panels. So far more than 6,700 women have been trained in advanced solar maintenance, enabling them to become full-time specialists who travel around the country to service clients.[58] Similarly, in India the solar engineering program at "Barefoot College" has trained hundreds of women across eight states to install and maintain solar power plants. Likewise, micro-hydro programs in Nepal and Pakistan have also been implemented by village-level functional groups that demand the equal participation of women.

2.4 Girls and Water

United Nations Sustainable Development Goal (SDG) 6 is universal access to clean water and sanitation for all. This is to address four billion people around the world who face severe water scarcity during least one month of the year.[59] Moreover, half a billion people globally face severe water scarcity all year round.

Females face additional significant challenges related to water. Because there is no toilet at home, girls and women around the world collectively spend 266 million hours every day to find a place to go.[60] This is disgraceful given the technological advancement human beings have made. Indeed, today, there are more mobile phones than toilets (see Figure 7).[61]

Similarly, girls and women collectively lose 200 million hours every day hauling water to their homes.[62] "It is women, especially the poorest women in low-income and middle-income countries, who bear disproportionate

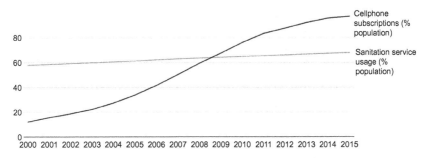

Figure 7 Global trends in mobile phones and sanitation services.
Source: [61]

Figure 8 Women carrying water in Singair, Bangladesh.
Source: Benjamin Sovacool, used with permission.

responsibility for water-related tasks, including water carrying, cooking, and washing."[63] Figure 8 shows this gender bias in water collection in Bangladesh. Studies have found that the more time-intensive fetching water is, the more likely it is done by a girl or a woman, rather than a boy or a man.[64,65] Hauling water, which is very heavy, can also lead to extreme physical stress, including the risk of diseases, heat stress, injury, and even death. [66]

Conversely, the provision of water and even the efficiency of water infrastructure projects work better when women are involved and empowered.[67] Better representation and involvement of women in water projects also leads to more productive generation activities and better implementation and management of water projects. Through these processes, women can also learn about hygiene and practices that enhance their health (linking with Section 2.6). For example, in India, under the National Rural Drinking Water Program, a community centered program provided sustainable access to drinking water by focusing exclusively on women. There, women benefited from a "healthy home survey," which then led to increased awareness about cleaner homes and safer water practices.[67] In Sri Lanka, a similar community participation model led to an enhanced drinking water supply for everyone (not just women) as well as more self-reliance and resilience among communities and economic empowerment.[68] The education and empowerment of women has also led to better water outcomes, and health outcomes, in Nepal[69] and more effective and participatory community-based water governance in Uganda with expanded access to water and improved health.[70]

2.5 Girls, Education, and Economic Opportunity

Today, more girls and young women than ever before are going to school – more than their mothers, their grandmothers, and generations before them. This improvement can be seen by the seventy-nine million more girls who are attending school today than in 1998.[71]

And yet, this still leaves 129 million girls not in school – approximately 32 million who are primary school age, 30 million who are lower-secondary school age, and 67 million who are upper-secondary school age.[71]

Representation of girls and women in STEM is worse, as Figure 9 indicates. What's at the root of disparity in STEM? Some, including leaders of powerful institutions, have made dubious claims that men are more intellectually brilliant or inherently talented than women.[72] Indeed, outdated mindset and stereotypes are a stubborn source of the inequality that permeates and persists in our society.[73] Graves and colleagues go so far as to argue that "the history of the scientific enterprise demonstrates that it has supported gender, identity, and racial inequity" and "its institutions have allowed discrimination, harassment, and personal harm of racialized persons and women." Big data and machine learning approaches have even confirmed that negative gender stereotypes about women are reflected in internet searches, which "leads people to think and act in ways that reinforce societal inequality, suggesting a cycle of bias propagation between society, artificial intelligence, and [internet] users.[74,75] And yet strong evidence shows

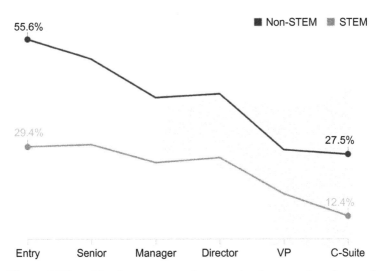

Figure 9 Disparities in access to science, technology, engineering, and medicine (STEM) occupations, 2023.

Source: [24]

the opposite, that for economies and universities to really thrive, the ranks of women working in science need to dramatically increase.[76]

The goal to achieve inclusive, gender-balanced STEM classrooms is not difficult. Many young, passionate, female scientists exist who are bright and curious about the world, and who want to harness STEM tools to promote sustainability objectives. Many of these girls, who may come from African and Indigenous heritage, even want to transform their communities by pursuing careers in science.[77] There are vital reasons to involve more girls in STEM. Evidence suggests that when educational institutions, especially schools, ignore gender inequalities, they fail to achieve their objectives and neglect the opportunity for women to transform their societies.[31]

So why else are girls not in school, and why don't they pursue careers in science or engineering? Simply put, gender inequality. Currently, only 49 percent of countries in the world have achieved gender parity – and this is just in primary education.[78] As the education level goes up, the disparity becomes greater, resulting in only 24 percent parity in upper secondary. This means sixty-seven million female teenagers are not in school.

Now, just imagine if your teenage girl isn't in school. The consequences are many and devastating. At the individual level, she is not receiving education for mental as well as social and emotional development. The impact on society is even more severe – increased poverty, child marriage, and the magnification of sociocultural norms, which exacerbate gender-based violence. Furthermore, conflict, war, the climate crisis, pandemic – all humanitarian crises – compound the reality of the sexist social and cultural norms that keep girls out of school.

The transformative power of girls' education – at the individual, national, and global levels – is undisputable and well documented. Today, we know that better educated females are more likely to be knowledgeable about food, nutrition, health and health care, childbearing and child raising, and even better caretakers of our planet, decreasing the carbon footprint of their family and their community. Foremost, education is the great equalizer of the formal labor market and enables higher earning potential. In fact, the World Bank estimated that our failure to ensure that the world's girls receive twelve years of education is costing US$15–$30 trillion in lost lifetime productivity and earnings.[79] Moreover, the global economy is losing out on a whopping US$160 trillion due to the gender pay gap throughout adulthood.[80] Similarly, the consulting firm McKinsey and Company estimated that advancing women's equality in the workforce could add between $12 trillion and $28 trillion to the global economy by 2025, or 26 percent of the annual global gross domestic product.[81]

This is because what girls and young women earn doesn't stay just with them. They contribute 90 percent of their earnings to their families and communities compared to about 35 percent of male contribution.[82] Economic growth isn't the only benefit of investing in girls. Educated girls have healthier and fewer children – factors that dramatically improve global health, population control, *and* climate change.[83] Women moreover invest on average more of their earnings than men do in their family's well-being – as much as ten times more. This is why philanthropist Melinda Gates has targeted women as the primary recipients of aid from the Gates Foundation: "The upshot is that a woman or a girl with some measure of power is busy improving her community in myriad ways. So, it makes sense to invest in development outcomes by investing in the women who are driving them every day."[9]

Yet rather than target this potential, many countries actively restrict it. The World Bank reports that women face unfair job restrictions in most of the countries examined (100 of 173 countries monitored), half of the countries monitored do not grant paternity leave (placing the burden of childcare solely on women), and they cannot even work at night in twenty-nine countries.[84]

Girls' education is also a powerful social transformation tool – including ending child marriage. According to Girls Not Brides, a global partnership committed to ending child marriage, every year, fifteen million girls are married before their eighteenth birthday. This equates to one girl getting married off every two seconds. However, if she were in school, particularly secondary school, every additional year would decrease the likelihood of her getting married off by six percentage points.[79]

2.6 Girls and Health

Girls' education also has a transformative impact on family and community health – reducing child and maternal morbidity and mortality, improving child health, and lowering fertility by using contraception, marrying later, having fewer children, and being better informed about the nutritional and other needs of children. Indeed, girls' education is the most effective tool for family planning, which in turn is one of the most impactful tools for climate adaptation and resilience.

And yet, of all young people living with HIV, 61 percent are females.[85] Yes, like all humanitarian crises, HIV/AIDS is also sexist and directly related to power. Furthermore, despite the fact that female genital mutilation (FGM), or female circumcision, is a human rights violation today, it still practiced in thirty-one countries, violating one in every three adolescent girls (fifteen to nineteen-year-olds).[86] Figure 10 shows data from UNICEF estimating that female genital mutilation/cutting has been done to more than 125 million girls and women in

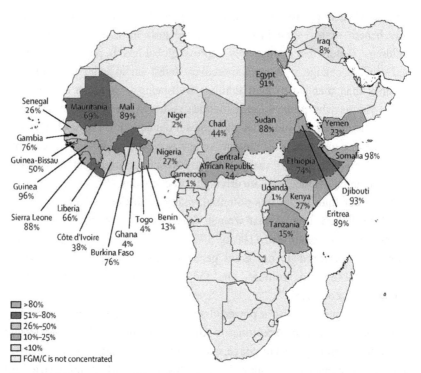

Figure 10 Prevalence of female genital mutilation or cutting among girls and
women aged fifteen to forty-nine by country.

Source: [87]

the twenty-nine countries in Africa and the Middle East where the practice is
concentrated, with the practice being nearly universal in Somalia, Guinea,
Djibouti, and Egypt.[87]

FGM is a grave health issue and a form of gender-based violence. Immediate
health consequences include bacterial and viral infections and obstetrical
complications.[87,88] These cost some countries, such as Egypt, more than
$3.7 million in health costs per year. But the damage extends far beyond the
financial. Girls undergoing FGM suffer severe pain, shock, hemorrhaging, and
ulceration of the entire genital region, as well as more serious infections such as
tetanus, sepsis, or even HIV/AIDS when instruments are not properly cleaned
between procedures.[89] Longer-term consequences include cysts and abscesses,
keloid scar formation, damage to the urethra, difficulty urinating, dyspareunia
(painful sexual intercourse), and sexual dysfunction,[89] plus mental illness, including post-traumatic stress disorder.[90,91] Female genital mutilation also increases the
risk of maternal death, stillbirths, and complications during pregnancy, especially
long-term maternal morbidity via vesicovaginal fistula. Most insidiously, in some

situations FGM can lead to complications that result in death, or infant death when girls become pregnant.[92]

Once again, girls and women can play a transformative role in changing these perniciously poor health outcomes. One powerful example is a CARE program in Bangladesh. It discovered that health and nutrition programs were radically more effective at reducing malnutrition among children when households also participated in activities that contributed to women's empowerment. To achieve this goal, the CARE program founded self-help groups of women and adolescent girls. These self-help groups had a ripple affect across communities and the nation, leading to a reduction in gender-based violence, an increase in awareness about the need for education, improved literacy, and enhanced decision-making power.[93] The underappreciated contribution of women to health care is vast, given that many young women play critical roles caring for family members or volunteering in the community. One global assessment of thirty-two countries representing 52 percent of the world's population estimated that the unrecognized value of women's contribution to the global health system was more than $3 trillion![94]

2.7 Girls, Violence, and National Security

Gender-based violence is one of the most insidious and pervasive human rights violations. These dehumanizing acts crosscut race, income, culture, and country. Although some may be misguided, focusing on the type of violence, for example, seeing sex as the problem of sexual violence, at the root of all gender-based violence is power – the imbalance and the abuse of power.

Who has power is predicted in utero, as the Introduction already explained. It's how our world has become grossly gender imbalanced with so many extra males. With this said, in the twenty-first century, we are experiencing a decreasing trend with legislation banning sex-selective abortions and increased cultural awareness of the value of girls.

And yet, until there is a global awakening, the shortage of females will also exacerbate every other kind of violence and humanitarian crisis. For example, the *Global Report on Trafficking in Person 2018* produced by the UN Office of Drugs and Crime reports that the overall number of reported trafficking victims has increased globally.[95] Trafficking of human beings is a form of modern slavery and one of the most profitable crimes with $150 billion in annual profit.[96] It includes sex slavery and bride trafficking, of which 99 percent of victims are girls and women.[97] On any given day, some 40.3 million people live as victims of modern day slavery, and a staggering 28.7 million are female – that's 71 percent – 20 percent of whom are girls.[98] As Figure 11 indicates, not all

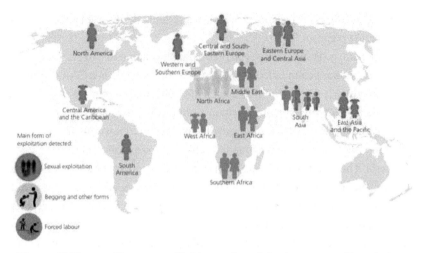

Figure 11 Forms of human trafficking and exploitation reported by victims.
Source: [95]

of this trafficking is sexually related. In some places such as Europe and North America, the exploitation is sexual, but in North Africa it takes the form of begging, and in Eastern Europe, the Middle East, and sub-Saharan Africa, forced labor.

Indeed, modern slavery is profitable. It is burgeoning all kinds of criminal ventures. For example, Using technology and social media like Facebook and WhatsApp, ISIS pimps a girl for $8,000.[99] Strategically using contraception to avoid pregnancy, they can sell and rape a girl, over and over again.

In fact, the gross gender imbalance may be jet-fueling the widespread violence in the world. One creditable data source is the Global Peace Index (GPI) produced by the Institute for Economics and Peace. Covering 99.7 percent of the world's population, GPI reports regional and global conflicts are accelerating.[100] The outcome is increased deaths from global conflict by 96 percent.[100] Moreover, the Middle East and North Africa have the most conflict. Not surprisingly, this region is also the most gender-imbalanced region in the world.

Gender-based violence is a pandemic and an endemic societal illness. Thus, ending it requires a wake-up call to see it as a public health emergency, with intervention and prevention targeting a paradigm shift in social and cultural norms. First, whether sexual harassment, domestic violence, or date rape, all forms of gender-based violence, are about power and control. Second, from Nairobi to New York, regardless of economic status, race, or culture, the single greatest challenge facing today's young women across the globe is violence against women. This insidious virus is amplified in conflict and war, as heinous crimes such as sex slavery to terrorists and rape as weapon of war are increasing. Consider the following acts of gender violence by region:

- Rape and domestic violence in South Asia: India, Pakistan, and Nepal.
- Ongoing war, forced/early marriage and sexual harassment in the Middle East: Iraq, Egypt, Jordan, and Morocco.
- Poverty and domestic violence in sub-Saharan Africa: Madagascar, Kenya, Zimbabwe, Trinidad, and Malawi.
- Gender discrimination, and social pressure to "marry before 30," to "handle both family and work," and "to look perfect" in China.
- Glass ceiling, media messages, and social expectation to "be and look perfect" in cities of Western countries: NYC, Boston, Montreal, London, and Paris.

Therefore, national security is inextricably linked to the safety of girls and women.[101] In fact, the best predictor of a nation at war is not lack of democracy, poverty, or religious or ethnic conflict. It is violence against women.[102] Similarly in the United States, a felony domestic violence conviction is the single most significant predictor of future violent crime.[103]

2.8 Momentum for Girls Empowerment

For Girls Glocal Leadership (4GGL) collected *the first-ever* women's empowerment data on a global scale. As a 501c3 charitable organization, as well as a social change movement, focusing on the next generation of women changemakers and peacebuilders, the target group was females eighteen to thirty-two years old. With this said, we also heard the voices of males (same age bracket) in order to be more inclusive, comprehensive, and representative of the millennial generation.

The global millennial women's empowerment data was collected in 2014 in five languages: English, French, Spanish, Chinese, and Arabic. It spanned six continents: Africa, Asia, Australia, Europe, and North and South Americas. The voices were natives of the countries, as well as diasporas living in another country, mainly the United States.

The aim was to understand the agency of today's young women – stemming not from external factors like education and jobs but from internal control and capacity achieved through *voice and choice*. Moreover, we also wanted to learn what lies in their hearts – their deepest fears, desires, hopes, and dreams.

Here are some sample questions:

- What does it mean for you to use your voice? Do you use it and how?
- How much control do you have in (various areas of) your life?
- What would you like to change the most in your life?
- Who contributes the most to making that change?
- If you have made changes in your life, how did you do it? What caused the change?
- Who supports you to use your voice and/or to make changes in your life?
- What is the most important issue to you and other young women in your society?

The results were deeply insightful. To begin, here are some fast facts about today's young women's use of voice and choice. Now more than ever, millennial women use their voices to bring about change. And with the prevalence of technology in both economically rich and poor countries, they use blogs and social media to create campaigns, share ideas, and fight for equality and justice – for themselves and others.

Furthermore, now more than ever before, today's young women have more choices, access, and opportunities in their lives. With this said, the level varies widely, with many young women in South Asia, sub-Saharan Africa, and the Middle East still struggling for basic rights, freedom, and dignity. As Table 2 indicates, girls are less concerned with physical appearance and love

Table 2 Conceptions of self-change and empowerment among a sample of girls

Q: Want to change the most?	Africa	China	Middle East	South Asia	Caribbean	US, EU, AU
Personal development	1st	2nd	1st	1st	2nd	1st
Career and income	2nd	1st	2nd	2nd	1st	2nd
Local mindset about women			3rd	2nd		
Relationship	3rd					3rd
Physical appearance		3rd		3rd		

Source: Author.

relationship, and far more concerned with personal development and career prospects and altering local mindsets about women.

Similarly, millennial women have more control and agency in their lives – with the most in education, the least in career. Ironically, family and partners are the greatest encouragers, as well as the greatest discouragers to young women creating changes in their lives and for others. In the next section, we will hear seven such inspiring stories of empowerment in the real world.

3 Stories: Harnessing Girl Power for Sustainability

From climate change to democracy, gender-based violence to the Ukraine war, girls around the world are harnessing and flexing the muscles of empowerment to accelerate societal change and promote justice. This section showcases seven case studies and models of girls' empowerment, focused on seven key global challenges, and dimensions of sustainability. Figure 12 offers an overview of these seven cases. Each case study follows the same structure of (1) offering an illustrative quote of the case study as well as a drawing of the case study commissioned by the Element, before (2) presenting a story that summarizes how action began, (3) discussing solutions to the sustainability challenge involved, and (4) articulating the broader national or even global importance of the issue being raised.

Empowerment Muscle	Description	Example
Focus	Pay particular attention to, a center of activity, attraction, or attention	*Focused attention of Greta Thunberg for climate justice*
Solidarity	Undivided, unity that is derived from being connected with a common purpose	*Fearless warriors of Hong Kong Pro-Democracy Movement*
Hope	Having faith in or believing that something better or greater will aspire	*Aspiration of Fatemah Qaderyan for STEM education*
Courage	From Latin *cor* "heart," quality of mind, heart and spirit that enables a person to face great difficulty, danger despite fear	*The courage of Chibok girls against terrorism*
Advocacy	Public support of a cause, particularly for others	*Girls behind #NeverAgain Movement for Gun Control*
Endurance	Power to withstand difficulty, challenges	*Determination of Nada al-Ahdal against child marriage, for educatioi*
Healing	To restore to wholeness, oneness	*Holistic healing of Ukrainian girls from gender-based violence of war*

Figure 12 Seven case studies of Girl Power and environmental, economic, social, or political sustainability.

Source: Author.

3.1 Case Study 1: Focus and Determination of Greta Thunberg for Climate Justice

Asperger's is my superpower . . . it has affected everything. If I did not have Asperger's and if I were not so strange, I would be stuck in this social game that everyone else seems to be so infatuated with. It makes me function a bit differently. I see the world in a different way, from a different perspective.

—Greta Thunberg

Focus is a superpower. Particularly in today's multitasking, multi-technology, incessantly noise-filled world, focusing our attention solely on one task or a person seems nearly impossible. In fact, we have normalized splitting our attention – with the word "multitasking" – believing "it's just the way it is," unable to change our destiny.

However, not focusing or splitting our attention has consequences. Allowing ourselves to be in a perpetual cycle of various thoughts, interruptions, and distractions, we're unable to return to tasks or people we set out to focus on, failing to follow through and complete tasks, thoroughly.

Indeed, focus is required in our lives, particularly in creating long-lasting and sustainable change. And Greta Thunberg (drawn in Figure 13) models this ability, extraordinarily. At just fifteen years young, she became the voice and inspiration to others in the global fight for climate justice. By being well versed in the field – with profound knowledge of scientific data, as well as practicing and modeling a lifestyle of "reduce, reuse, recycle," including zero or low carbon footprint travel – Greta has had an impact that even the most seasoned climate experts and activists have not had. Focused on one goal – to persuade

Figure 13 A drawing of climate activist Greta Thunberg.
Source: Drawn for the Element by Gabriela Cordero Durán, used with permission.

the world to listen to climatologists and for nations to align with the Paris Climate Accords – she has and will remain steadfast and determined in this mission. As she said, "Instead of worrying about how that future might turn out, I'm going to try to change that future while I still can."[104]

3.1.1 Herstory: How It All Began

Greta Thunberg was born in Stockholm, Sweden, on January 3, 2003, to opera singer Malena Ernman and actor Svante Thunberg. Born and raised in one of the most developed nations in the world, Greta's ecosystem provides care and support to their citizens that other nations only dream of. For starters, Sweden is an economically developed and socially advanced nation with one of the world's best education system. Sweden also provides universal health care for all, with the option of adding private supplemental coverage if individuals choose. Another social norm and societal support the Swedes receive is 480 days, or 16 months, of parental leave per child – an unimaginable reality for people in many other countries.

Thus, it is not surprising that Sweden, along with other Scandinavian countries, consistently ranks at the top in gender equality. The Swedish government models equality with female-majority ministers as well as being the very first nation to adopt a feminist foreign policy.

Even with this extraordinary social, economic, and political ecosystem, Greta has not had an easy life. She was diagnosed with Asperger's syndrome, a condition on the autism spectrum that is experienced in only 1–2 percent of the world population. Even more rare are females with Asperger's – only one in four. Thus, Greta Thunberg possesses something only 0.25 percent of the world has!

So, who are these rare human beings?

According to the Asperger's Autism Network, those with Asperger's often have above-average intelligence, focus, and memory. They are likely to be detailed oriented and more likely to be gifted with a fair and just disposition. Simultaneously, they may struggle with regulating emotions, anxiety, and impulses. Foremost, they have the opposite habit of most of us – difficulty with losing focus.

With this said, there are great disparities between Asperger's males and females in diagnosis and treatment from health care providers, as well as from society at-large. For example, females are less likely to be correctly diagnosed with Asperger's. Instead, they are more likely to be misdiagnosed with something else, like a psychological mood disorder, rather than a neurological developmental disorder such as Asperger's. This is largely due to the fact that health care professionals are trained to recognize typical Asperger's/autism spectrum expression in males with little or no knowledge, nor special training for identifying symptoms in females.

Undiagnosed, misdiagnosed, or misunderstood gender perception of autism can leave girls with Asperger's feeling alone. Developing friendship can be difficult, and in many cases, girls with autism face bullying.

This is what Greta experienced and endured. Feeling alone as an "outsider looking in," Greta fell into a deep depression at age eleven when she learned about the climate crisis and the devastating impact of human behaviors on our planet. She deeply felt the pain and suffering of Mother Earth as she read and learned – obsessively – about the problem. Flooded with the doom and gloom knowledge, it evoked fear.

3.1.2 Solution: Fridays for Future and School Strikes

Then, Greta did something powerful. She merely changed her focus from the problem to the solution and action! What she didn't know at the time was that her extraordinary ability to focus is her superpower. It would lead her to become not only a world renowned climate justice warrior but also a feminist icon.

On September 9, 2018, Greta began a silent protest. Armed with just a cardboard sign that read *"Skolstrejk* for *Klimatet"* (School Strike for Climate), Greta took a bold stand – literally standing alone outside of the Swedish Parliament. She had one and only one goal: to change Sweden's environmental policies and the *mindset* of incoming parliamentarians on the climate crisis. With focus and determination, she returned to the exact same spot every single Friday. Even though she had to skip school for her stand, she continued without fail.

Soon, Greta's action went viral. The image of her and her sign outside Parliament ignited what is now known as #FridaysForFuture: a youth-led, youth-organized global movement on all continents with members in more than 7,500 cities. Her actions sparked a historically large youth movement, leading to a series of school strikes coordinated in September 2019 across the world. An incredible 7.6 million people participated in this single strike across 185 countries, involving 6,135 distinct events, 73 trade unions, 3,024 businesses, and 820 organizations, making it "one of the largest environmental social movements" ever.[105] Schoolchildren and students participated alongside adults and other activist leaders with protests taking place across urban areas and national capitols, university campuses, and village greens, with many organizations and corporations allowing, and even encouraging, their employees to take part.

Greta's focus and steadfast action to persuade Parliament to acknowledge climate scientists inspired others to join. Thus, building and amplifying a collective voice, Greta's stand grew and magnified. Throughout it all, her focus remained the same: for policymakers to acknowledge the climate science and take action towards tangible steps to align their nations and the broader international community with the Paris Accord.

Today, Greta has a global platform with presence, power, and credibility with which to influence the world. Although she continues to target her own government, she also has the attention of the United Nations. In fact, she does not shy away from speaking directly to the UN on its own lack of knowledge of IPCC data and, foremost, inaction. She scolds UN policymakers on how they have stolen her childhood and the future of generations to come. "Our house is on fire!"

Indeed, focused action is truly Greta's superpower. And she shares this power with every individual, community, nation, and international entity in order to avert the climate crisis. Now.

In fact, though Greta's voice has become a megaphone, what many people may not see is another trait and gift – humility. Yes, Greta is humble – a rare currency in today's self-glorifying, "selfie" culture. Her inner and outer modesty is obvious. Dressed in down-to-earth clothing, she genuinely does not seek attention. In fact, she hides from the spotlight. When she speaks, she states that it is not her but the scientists – like IPCC and other climate experts the politicians have long ignored – they should listen to. Greta's humility to amplify the voice of experts, not hers, strengthens her ability to persuade and promote real action.

However, Greta knows the power of her voice. She uses it wisely with targeted speeches that, again, highlight her incredible attention to detail and focus in all that she does. And as a true "empower-ist," she empowers the voices of others, particularly youth. "[The adults] are hopeful that the young people are going to save the world, but we are not. There is simply not enough time to wait for us to grow up and become the ones in charge."[106]

Greta's focus and action for our planet never waivers. Even during the COVID-19 pandemic, she continued the Friday School Strike for Climate, virtually. Furthermore, as the inaugural Gulbenkian Prize for Humanity recipient, she gave away her award prize money of one million euros to charitable actions that are combating the climate crisis.

3.1.3 The Issue: Climate Change and Its Impact on Girls and Young Women

Climate change is sexist. That is, the devastating impact of global warming is disproportionately experienced by girls and women.

According to the World Health Organization, women and children are *four-teen times* more likely to die than men during a natural disaster caused by the effects of climate change. In fact, whenever there is a food shortage, girls and women are the first to go hungry. Furthermore, what many of us in highly industrialized, technology-driven countries may not realize is that women are the farmers in the developing world, accounting for anywhere between 45 and 80 percent of all food production, depending on the region. In fact, nearly two-thirds of the female labor force in developing countries – and more than 90 percent in many African countries – are in agriculture. Therefore, the climate crisis is also an economic crisis for them. Lastly, girls and women are more vulnerable to the effects of climate change than men simply because they are the majority of the world's poor. They also depend more on natural resources that are threatened by climate change for their livelihood. In sum, they face social, economic, *and* political barriers that limit their coping capacity.

Yes, girls and women are overwhelmingly more vulnerable to the detrimental consequences of climate change. And yet, *Girl Power* is also the single most impactful solution to mitigating this global crisis.

As was already mentioned in Section 2, according to Project Drawdown, an extensive group of climate researchers, scientists, business leaders, and policymakers, the empowerment of girls – most specifically, girls' education and family planning – is one of the most effective tools to stop greenhouse gases in the atmosphere *and* reduce them. For example, just by allowing one girl – yes, that's just *one girl* – to receive an additional year of schooling, a nation's resilience to climate disasters can be expected to improve, on average, by 3.2 points.

Furthermore, globally, women are the primary household caretakers, agricultural workers, and the group most vulnerable to violent conflict. Making them the central part of the solution, on the frontlines of the fight against climate change, is critical. When we educate and empower women with sustainable methods and options, they can generate the most effective impact in our global fight against climate change. Women are the heart of their communities. Their powerful voices in their communities make them important leaders in the fight against climate change.

As Greta says, the global climate crisis is a call to action for every one of us. It's a call for us to build our muscle of empowerment and take action for equitable change. And empowered girls like Greta are demonstrating how.

Data from hundreds of scientific organizations, foundations, and nonprofits predict irreversible damage to our planet if we do not act now. The National Aeronautics and Space Administration (NASA) reports a greater than 95 percent probability that the current warming trends are related solely to human activity.

In fact, the warming trend has led to a 1.62 degree increase in global temperature since the nineteenth century. These temperatures peaked from 2010 to 2015 and continue to trend upwards. These temperatures have increased at such an exponential rate over the last century that they are likely to have been caused solely by human behavior and activity.

"Reduce, Reuse, Recycle" is the motto, and changing human behavior is precisely what Greta is focused on. According to NASA, there are two main actions individuals can do right now:

1. Reduce emissions of greenhouse gases in the atmosphere.
2. Adapt to the current environment by creating sustainable methods of energy to stabilize the levels we currently have.

In practical terms, this means we can:

1. Travel smarter by choosing lower-emission transportation modes.
2. Eat food containing a lower carbon footprint (i.e. local seasonal fruits and vegetables and locally prepared foods as opposed to those flown from across the world or grown in heated greenhouses).
3. Recycle and shop from sustainable clothing brands.
4. Reduce single-use nonbiodegradable items like plastic.

Every single one of us can do these simple actions. Now. With focus and determination like Greta, we can restore and heal our planet from human-created devastation and consumption.

3.2 Case Study 2: Solidarity of Fearless Warriors of Hong Kong Pro-Democracy Movement

Be like water!
—Hong Kong protesters

Solidarity is vital fuel for the longevity and sustainability of movements. It's how words like "Me Too" – two of the most powerful words in the English language that exude solidarity and empathy – can ignite a wildfire movement across the United States of America and around the world.

Unknown to many westerners, a powerful solidarity movement ignited in the East. For freedom, democracy, and sovereignty, the people of Hong Kong (or Hongkongers) are united in solidarity fighting one of the most powerful governments – China.

Like the people of most nations, all Hongkongers want is simply autonomy and self-governance. And their vital fuel for accomplishing this insurmountable task against China is solidarity. In today's divisive, polarized world, with many nations inflamed and engulfed in partisanship, civil strife, and culture wars within themselves, eroding trust and tearing down democracy, Hongkongers are in fact galvanizing and using their superpower – solidarity – for democracy. Regardless of age, gender, or class, the entire city-state of Hong Kong is in solidarity for freedom from the oppression of China.

With this said, one particular demographic group is even more exemplary, going beyond the call of duty. This fearless and heroic cohort is the adolescent girls and young women of Hong Kong – at the forefront of the protests, serving as a human shield for the rest of their fellow protesters. Their self-sacrificing action protects other protesters, allowing them to forge ahead or, if needed, escape without arrest by or injury from the pro-China police. Indeed, they are today's real-life ninja warriors, not only demonstrating the power of solidarity for Hong Kong but also modeling women's empowerment (see Figure 14).

3.2.1 Herstory: How It All Began

The herstory of Hong Kong goes back to 1997 when the Basic Law was created and established in the hand-over of Hong Kong from its 150-year colonial-ruler, United Kingdom, to China. For the next fifty years (1997–2047), the law

Figure 14 A drawing of the Hong Kong democracy protesters.
Source: Drawn for the Element by Gabriela Cordero Durán; used with permission.

would allow "one country, two systems." This means, free from China's communist government and economic system, Hong Kong could continue its capitalist system and liberated way of life. Furthermore, the law set out the sources of law, the relationship between Hong Kong and the Central Government (State Council), the fundamental rights and duties of Hong Kong residents, and the branches of local government.[107]

Then in 2019, Hong Kong's very own Chief Executive, Carrie Lam, proposed an amendment to the law, allowing extradition of criminal suspects to mainland China. Simply, this meant that suspects including political dissents, activists, and journalists would undergo unfair trials and violent treatment in China. Moreover, this would erode Hong Kong's legal system and its built-in safeguards, giving China greater power over Hong Kong.[108]

3.2.2 Solution: Sustained Democracy Protests

On March 15, 2019, the streets of Hong Kong were electrified with people power. Blanketing the whole city-state of Hong Kong, Hongkongers were willing to risk their lives for freedom and democracy, against the almighty China (see Figure 14). It spread like wildfire, and in three months, it galvanized over two million people in Hong Kong. Demonstrating the superpower of solidarity, the protest transformed into a pro-democracy, universal suffrage movement.

Initially, the protest was about just one ultimatum: the withdraw of the Extradition Bill. However, when Carrie Lam was not responsive, the protest grew and amplified, uniting around "five demands, not one less":[109]

1. Not to be classified as a "riot."
2. Amnesty for arrested protesters.
3. An independent inquiry into police brutality.
4. Universal suffrage.
5. Withdrawal of the Extradition Bill.

As the longest and the most widespread movement in Hong Kong – easily surpassing the three-month Umbrella Revolution of 2014 when Hong Kong then protested against China for their interference in Hong Kong's candidates in its election – this solidarity movement made history. Furthermore, the Extradition Bill has been dropped, evolving the movement into a much wider call for change by Hongkongers against China.

With this said, there were setbacks. Fifteen high-profile protesters were arrested by the Hong Kong Administration.[110] Furthermore, China cracked down, introducing a new national security law[111] to diminish Hong Kong's autonomy and punish protesters.

3.2.3 The Issue: Girl Power in Democracy

The power of this Hong Kong pro-democracy movement can be attributed to three distinct and unique practices – all centered around solidarity. In fact, these practices may be a model for today's movement building.

First, this movement is operationalized as a leaderless organ. Without one central leader or a core group of leaders with a hierarchical structure for the opposition to target and defeat, the movement continued and could exist anywhere.

The second practice is related to the first – fluidity. With their proverbial ethos, *Be water*[112] – formless and shapeless like water – the movement practices dynamism and adaptability anywhere, everywhere. For instance, youth organizers use social media and innovative technology that democratizes voting mechanisms on various platforms in order to organize protests anywhere. And their quick and concise planning has thwarted the opposition, which uses traditional tools and methods. In fact, even the COVID-19 pandemic couldn't stop the Hong Kong pro-democracy movement. Using innovative online tools, they held asynchronous demonstrations inspiring and empowering nontraditional groups to be part of Hong Kong's freedom movement from anywhere, including mainland China.[113]

One such nontraditional group is made of the adolescent girls and young women of Hong Kong.[114] Debunking the traditional belief of males, especially young males, as the heroes at the frontline of the battle fields, the young freedom fighters of this movement are adolescent girls. Redefining heroism and power, they are a powerful model of *Girl Power* – a new generation of political justice warriors igniting, leading, and supporting social and political movements around the world.

This brings us to the third distinct and unique practice of this Hong Kong pro-democracy movement – one that is powerfully modeled by *Girl Power*. Although the Hong Kong protesters have made some global headlines, there is no personal stardom or individual celebrity in the movement. Contrary to the West's obsession with fame, notoriety, and selfie culture, this *Girl Power* embodies anonymity rooted in solidarity.

Disguised in makeshift tear-gas masks and black hoods, these bold, faceless warriors are real-life democracy activists who run toward the police in order to protect their fellow protesters behind them. It is indeed solidarity with their fellow Hongkoners that is empowering these young freedom fighters. Their goal isn't just to rewrite their own individual herstories. They aspire to rewrite the collective Hong Kong herstory.

Thus, hair pulled back in high ponytails, clad in their black protest uniforms with tear-gas masks over their faces, adolescent girls and young women – as young as 15-year-olds – are at the frontline of the protests, facing the opposition head-on. Individually, each superheroine could be removed, easily. Alone, she would be pushed aside by the police. But together in solidarity – mentally, spiritually, and physically with linked arms – they serve as a human shield and barricade for their fellow demonstrators. Moreover, they are each other's greatest support, safety, and security.

While some have dismissed their efforts as a minor delay of the police, their presence and actions have worked. Their palpable and visual force has not only delayed the riot police but also prevented arrests and, foremost, allowed their fellow protesters to continue the fight.[115]

With this said, their heroic action comes at a tremendous cost. As the first-line defenders, they are more vulnerable to violence from the police, like getting hit by rubber bullets and tear-gas. They are also more likely to get arrested. Moreover, as young females, they face a great power disadvantage – physically and verbally – including threats, violence, and misogyny from the police.

Indeed, these protests have been rampant with accusations of abuse and violence against women – everything from humiliation, strip search, and trolling to assault, rape threats, and actual rape.[116] And violence against women doesn't happen in a vacuum. It is allowed and permeated in societies, particularly those that are deeply rooted in patriarchy and sexism. According to the Global Gender Gap Report 2023, at the current rate, it will take 189 years for the East Asia and Pacific region to reach gender parity (See Figure 3). Compare this, for instance, to Western Europe, where it will take sixty-seven years – or within an adolescent girl's lifetime – to reach parity.

Furthermore, the assumption that economic development will bring about gender equality and women's empowerment is simply not true. Hong Kong – and East Asia, with some of the most economically developed nations – still believes and very much practices traditional and outdated gender norms. For instance, girls and women are expected to be respectful, dutiful, and submissive. And sexist attitudes and messages also come from mainland China. For example, one of China's media campaigns paints the Hong Kong protesters as a "spoiled mistress that has been pampered for too long."[117] This demonstrates the dismissive and sexist manner in which China treats the people of Hong Kong. China's blatant display of sexism is a stark contrast to the Hong Kong protesters' liberation of girls and women – the old status quo versus a new vision, a new world.

3.3 Case Study 3: Hope and Aspiration of Fatemah Qaderyan for STEM Education

Night will not always rule over Afghanistan. A new day will come soon.
—Fatemah Qaderyan, 2018

Hope is an aspirational state of mind and being. In its lightest form, it can just be a belief that something better will transpire. In its strongest and most note-worthy form, it is an empowerment muscle that's exercised to alter the status quo. Furthermore, it fuels perseverance and endurance in times of great challenges. In fact, hope is most powerful when life seems dark. Hope is the light and fuel of the soul.

Unfortunately, many of us don't utilize this powerful muscle to its full extent. Some of us simply give up when we face a challenge, while the rest certainly do when faced with multiple difficulties. Rather than seeing hardship as an opportunity to exercise, build, and strengthen the empowerment muscle of hope, we let doubt and fear – including self-generated – take over control.

This is why we need models like Fatemah Qaderyan (see Figure 15). Despite the harsh reality Fatemah has faced – and continues to endure even today – she practices audacious hope. In fact, she believes in a brighter future, not just for herself but also for all girls in Afghanistan. Her action has paved the way for the next generation of Afghanistan to dream big and reach for the stars not just in STEM but also in every field.

In fact, this *Girl Power* may be more powerful and sustainable than the US military in bringing about profound change in war-torn countries like Afghanistan.

Figure 15 A drawing of Fatemah Qaderyan.
Source: Drawn for the Element by Gabriela Cordero Durán, used with permission.

And now that the United States and NATO forces have left this terrorist-controlled state, it is time to support and invest in the empowerment of Afghan youth, especially young women as leaders and changemakers in Afghanistan. Long-lasting change can only come from building agency and the capacity of the local people – starting with adolescent girls and young women.

3.3.1 Herstory: How It All Began

According to the Thomson Reuters Foundation, Afghanistan is the second most dangerous country in the world for girls and women (see Figure 16).[118] This comes from assessing six danger or risk categories females face: access to health and health care, access to economic resources, customary practices, sexual violence, nonsexual violence, and human trafficking. Afghanistan ranked *the worst* in three of them: access to general health care and all forms of violence, including sexual violence.

This dark backdrop makes Fatemah's herstory and her superpower – hope – even more extraordinary. In one of the poorest countries on the planet, where most people expect the worst, the light of hope shines even more brightly.

In fact, Fatemah Qaderyan was born and raised in Herat, Afghanistan. As the first city to be captured by the Taliban, her birthplace has been marred by decades of civil war and terrorism. The Taliban continues to violate the human rights of its people, especially of girls and women.

3.3.2 Solution: A Robotics Team in Afghanistan

Despite Fatemah's challenging environment, she has found a way to survive and thrive. Her superpower and the muscle of empowerment she models is hope.

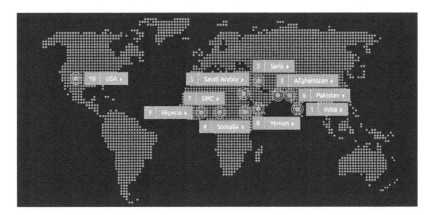

Figure 16 The world's ten most dangerous countries for women.
Source: [118]

Believing in the greatness of Afghan girls' empowerment, she takes action to fight systemic gender oppression. At just fifteen years young, she was chosen to be on the *first-ever*, all-female robotics team in Afghanistan. With 150 applicants, the odds of being one of the chosen six were slim. But she had hope. Indeed, her hope for greatness led to being chosen again to be the captain of this elite team called the Afghan Dreamers.

The real test of the strength of her hope empowerment muscle came shortly thereafter. The Afghan Dreamers were invited to compete in the 2017 International Robotics Championships in Washington, DC, for creating a robot that distinguishes between contaminated and clean water, a vital invention for a country like Afghanistan that continues to experience war, conflict, and terrorism that destroys the infrastructure for clean water. And with the support of Roya Mahboob, Afghanistan's first tech CEO and a longtime supporter of girls' education, the Afghan Dreamers were on their way to Washington, DC.

This was when Fatemah's superpower was tested. The United States Embassy in Kabul, Afghanistan, denied their visas – not once, but twice. Moreover, in order to make a plea Fatemah traveled to the Embassy herself from her hometown – an approximately 530-mile journey with dangerous road conditions most people in developed economies can't imagine, in addition to passing through Taliban territory.[119,120] Notwithstanding, the Embassy remained firm on the denial.

Then, Fatemah took to social media. Blasting it to the world, she shared their unique and powerful story – the audacious hope of girls, living in one of the most dangerous countries in the world, for STEM education. And millions heard the call and amplified her plea. This attracted the attention of the president of the United States, who intervened. The US Department of Homeland Security granted the Afghan Dreamers a temporary "parole" status to visit the USA without a visa. And the Afghan Dreamers won the silver medal in the competition, a symbol of their exceptional knowledge and skill in science, as well as of their hope, endurance, and unwavering tenacity.

Sadly, back in their hometown of Herat, Afghanistan, the team's landmark achievement was not met with jubilee. On the contrary, the patriarchal power structure saw the girls' accomplishment and progress as a threat to their existing status quo. Furthermore, when the girls returned to schools, it was seen as sin by many in their province.

Nevertheless, Fatemah (and the Dreamers) forged on, eager to continue her education – hope for a better future. Indeed, unwavering hope drives her to show up at school, every day – a risky and courageous act most of us take for granted. And to show just how dangerous, a week after returning home from

Washington, DC, Fatemah woke up to the deafening noise of a bomb going off near her house. The thunderous sound also interrupted her mother's morning prayers. Soon, they realized it was a bomb exploding in a nearby mosque, the mosque where her father was for his morning prayers. As Fatemah processed what was happening, she immediately called her father. In her own words. "For the first time in my life, my father didn't answer my call."

Although her father was not killed in the initial blast, he died shortly thereafter from injuries. And just at the tender age of fifteen, Fatemah faced her deepest sorrow and fear. Believing in her and her right to education, her father was the staunchest supporter of her STEM education and robotics. And this powerful source of Fatemah's hope – in a culture that diminishes girls and their potential in society – was gone. Furthermore, shockingly, some members of her community blamed Fatemah for his death. They believed her participation in the robotics competition was the reason for the bombing.

When we face a great tragedy, we can easily give up our muscle-building training. This is why we need others to be the mirror, showing and reminding us who we truly are. For Fatemah, it was her mother. She encouraged her to stay with the Afghan Dreamers, reminding her of her *dreams* beyond her current reality.

Restoring hope, it gave Fatemah the fuel to endure one of the darkest moments in her life. She continued to lead her team, and this led her to partner with Roya Mahboob's Digital Citizen in order to build the first STEM education center in Kabul at the University of Afghanistan. Rather than hoping just for herself, she opened the doors for thousands, if not millions, of young Afghans – girls and boys alike – to pursue an education in STEM. She has been called *the* Afghan Dreamer, and this title only grazes the surface of her impact. Fatemah not only dreams but also, with hope, she believes that she can change her life, her country, and the world for the better.

3.3.3 The Issue: Gender Inequality in Education

Now that we have gotten our first taste of education,
we are determined to get as much as we can to build a brighter future for our country.
—Fatemah Qaderyan, 2018 Oslo Freedom Forum Speech

Fatemeh's generation makes up nearly two-thirds of the Afghan population. Of these vibrant youth, less than two-thirds of males and an even more dismal one-third of females are literate.[121] Another way to see this literacy poverty is UNICEF's estimate that of the 3.7 million Afghan children and youth, 60 percent of the girls are not in school due to the unstable, volatile, and violent environment in which they live.[122]

This is why Fatemah is a model of hope. Her practice in building the empowerment muscle of hope is extraordinary in the grim reality of Afghanistan – especially for girls. In fact, her practice of hope, dreams, and aspirations, not just for herself but for all girls in Afghanistan, is exceptional.

Today, STEM is the fastest growing area of research and jobs, worldwide. So access to STEM education and programs is critical for a nation like Afghanistan. And girls and young women are leading the way. Case in point: in response to the COVID-19 pandemic and Herat's lack of ventilators, the Afghan Dreamers made ventilator prototypes from used car parts. This is a testament to the power of STEM in a crisis and the power of hope for humanity.

Indeed, Fatemah hoped and dreamed even as a child. "Everything in a child starts with imagination. After a while, imagination becomes a dream, and once they have a dream, they want to achieve that dream in reality."[123] At the age of six, she was dreaming of a brighter future and "before she knew the dangers of dreaming in Afghanistan, [she spent her childhood] falling asleep with a book under her pillow, curious about everything. And it was her fascination with the inner workings of robots after seeing the movie 'Robots' for the first time, that left her with an unquenchable curiosity."[123]

3.4 Case Study 4: Extraordinary Courage of Chibok Girls Against Terrorism

We are the Chibok girls that have been in captivity, and now we are alive.
—Rebecca

Whether of a spider, public speaking, or heights, most human beings have fears. And yet, there are those who practice courage, even transforming and transcending horrific fear, in order to summon extraordinary action. One such example is the story of the Chibok girls (see Figure 17).

Galvanizing the globe with the outcry #BringBackOurGirls – which included notable individuals like Michelle Obama and Angelina Jolie and celebrities like Anne Hathaway and Salma Hayek – our world demanded the release of the 276 girls kidnapped by the militant Boko Haram from a boarding school in the Nigerian village of Chibok.

3.4.1 Herstory: How It All Began

On the brink of midnight of April 21, 2014, the Boko Haram militants, disguised as government military officials, invaded the small farming village of Chibok, Nigeria. During the invasion, the militants also kidnapped 276 girls from

Figure 17 A drawing of the Chibok girls.

Source: Drawn for the Element by Gabriela Cordero Durán, used with permission.

a boarding school, then forced them to watch their community and school burn.[124] If this wasn't enough, they terrorized the girls as they told them of their choices – either be taken as Boko Haram slaves or left in the school to burn.[124]

What the militants didn't consider was that there was another choice – run! Although the unknown of running through the Nigerian bushes may be frightening, the known, of becoming a sex slave for ruthless terrorists, was fatalistic and permanent.

In fact, Boko Haram made it clear why they abducted these particular girls – education. It's why they burned the school, so that other girls couldn't attend that school again. Furthermore, as Boko Haram's property, their sex slaves would spend the rest of their lives learning how to live under Sharia law. They would learn to become "dutiful Islamic women."

The prospect of these girls returning home was bleak. For one, no one knew where they were taken. Second, even the government wasn't able to confirm that they were taken by Boko Haram. In fact, the government seemed powerless against the terrorists, disregarding many of their heinous acts. Lastly, Chibok is a small farming community with no political power or influence. Thus, the return of the kidnapped girls seemed impossible.

3.4.2 Solution: Mothers Take Action With #BringBackOurGirls

Never say never, especially to committed mothers! With nothing but hope and faith, the mothers of the 276 abducted girls began #BringBackOurGirls when no one would help or listen. Lo and behold, #BringBackOurGirls became a movement, a global justice demand, receiving prominent support from girl champions like Michelle Obama and Malala Yousafzai, as well as Hollywood celebrities and pop stars like Beyoncé. This global attention pressured the Nigerian government to get a confirmation from Boko Haram that they had indeed kidnapped the Chibok girls.[125]

While the mothers relentlessly campaigned – every single day – to bring back their girls, the abducted girls, themselves, were forced into hell. Raped and tortured – over and over again – they were also forced to marry the rapists under the Boko Haram's law.[126] Others became child soldiers, female suicide bombers, and brutal killers. All girls were forced to convert to Islam.[127]

However, the resilience of the human spirit is extraordinary. Despite terror and inhumane conditions, the girls mustered up courage. Inextricably linked and connected together, they gave each other hope to survive.

In fact, patriarchy and toxic masculinity weren't new to the Chibok girls. Throughout their lives, they were taught males had the power, and females were to simply marry and be educated only to the point of being a good wife.

Thus, with extraordinary courage, some of the Chibok girls decided to run – for freedom and a future. Their remarkable courage is not found in their escape alone. It is found in their willingness to fight every day for a more empowered tomorrow.

3.4.3 The Issue: Extremists Target Girls and Young Women

There are still 112 girls reported missing.[128] Some are still held captive. Others are believed to be dead. And although UNICEF has reported that Boko Haram has kidnapped over 1,000 minors and killed over 2,000 teachers,[129] there's been relative silence on the subject.

Shockingly, the terrorism the Chibok girls experienced is not unique. Malala Yousafzai was shot by the Taliban. Nadia Murad and other Yazidi young women were sex slaves to ISIS.

In fact, girls and women around the world are disproportionately affected by terrorism and violent conflict. In the book *Sex & World Peace*, Hudson and colleagues state more girls and women have been killed in violent conflict than "all those lost during all the wars and civil strife of the twentieth century."[130] From Boko Haram to the Taliban, terrorists establish their power by subjugating those they perceive to be the weaker sex. They use sexual violence, forced marriage, denial of education, twisted religious teaching, and unimaginably violent tactics to suppress girls and women.[131] And the subjugation of girls and women benefits them in many ways, including financially. According to data from the Council on Foreign Relation, from recruitment to suicide attacks to income generation, more than six percent of all terrorist organizations have had women play some role in their activities.[132]

Terrorists purposefully and strategically target the weak and the vulnerable to display power and inflict terror – thus, terrorists. However, knowing stories like that of the Chibok girls can help bring awareness to the plight of girls and women in violent conflict.

3.5 Case Study 5: Inclusive Advocacy of #NeverAgain for Gun Control

Never live your life with the idea that you're only one person, and your voice doesn't matter.
—Jaclyn Corin

In today's self-absorbed selfie culture, focusing on and taking action for others as a mission and a cause is commendable. Moreover, when it's done inclusively, incorporating the voices of all groups impacted by the common injustice, it is even more powerful.

The powerful advocates of this herstory are ordinary girls (and boys) who discovered their superpower – inclusive advocacy – unfortunately after a great tragedy. The deadliest mass shooting at a high school in United States history, the gunman at Marjory Stoneman Douglas High School in Parkland, Florida, killed and stopped seventeen human lives – students and teachers. Determined to never let gun violence happen again, Emma Gonzalez, Sarah Chadwick, Sofie Whitney, and Jacyln Corin – along with their male allies Cameron Kasky, Alex Wind, and Alfonso Calderon – launched the #NeverAgain campaign (see Figure 18).

In solidarity, the community organized the largest single day of protest against gun violence in US history – March for Our Lives in Washington, DC – as well as hundreds of other sister marches across the US and around the world, as far as India and Japan.[133] These young justice warriors had a powerful mission: to harness the power of young people across the country to fight for sensible gun violence prevention policies that save lives.[134] And this mission wasn't just for them. They also supported and amplified unheard voices – young people facing everyday gun violence in the ghettos and other impoverished intercity neighborhoods. In the depths of their grief, they championed others just like them – a new generation of leaders rising across the nation.[135]

With this said, if you asked any one of them if they had envisioned themselves as advocates before that terrifying day, they would definitively say no. Their activism was thrust upon them. They were called to action.

Figure 18 A drawing of the girls behind the #NeverAgain campaign.

Source: Drawn for the Element by Gabriela Cordero Durán, used with permission.

3.5.1 Herstory: How It All Began

On Valentine's Day, February 14, 2018, the students at Marjory Stoneman Douglas High School (MSD) woke up to experience, not love, but their worst nightmare. At approximately 2:30 pm EST, police were dispatched to the school because an active mass shooter with an AR-15 semiautomatic had been identified. A nineteen-year-old male – shockingly, one of their classmates – was causing and spreading terror by shooting people for almost an hour. Outside the freshman building, two students were brutally shot. Another fifteen were viciously killed inside the building. In all, seventeen students and staff died on that Valentine's Day. Dozens more were wounded. Hundreds were locked down and terrorized, texting their loved ones their last words.[136]

Tragically, this terrifying school shooting is not an anomaly in America. In fact, shamefully, it has become the norm and a major fear in students' lives. And schools are not the only firing range for mass shootings. From synagogues to supermarkets, Americans now experience more mass shootings than days on the calendar.[137]

However, the story at MSD *is* unique. Determined not to have this horrifying incident define their story, as well as to honor the lives of the seventeen who died, the students, teachers, coaches, and staff of MSD galvanized to change the trajectory of their story *and* the future. Channeling their grief and pain along with the collective grief and pain of others who have also tragically faced gun violence, Emma, Sarah, Sofie, and Jaclyn, along with their male allies, ignited their peers' fight for social and policy change on guns.

3.5.2 Solution: March for Our Lives

Just days after the most traumatic day in their lives, Jaclyn Corin organized a bus to transport 100 Parkland students to Tallahassee, Florida, the state capital, using social media, press releases, and flyers to spread the news to other students and rally support.[138] The trip was *solely* organized by teenagers, and it had one purpose: to speak with state lawmakers and convince them to pursue common-sense gun reform.[139]

However, sadly, the adults – the lawmakers – disappointed them. They weren't just unwilling to help. They were in fact complicit in our nation's gun violence by voting not to take up a bill that would ban assault rifles. Watching the feckless behavior of the lawmakers in real life, the students decided to take action themselves.[141] Particularly, girls' activism was amplified.[140] Emma Gonzalez tweeted out that day, "Are you Kidding me ??? #NeverAgain We are not forgetting this come Midterm Elections – the Anger that I feel right now is indescribable."

On March 24, 2018, the young justice warriors of MSD organized the largest anti-gun violence protest in America.[141] Gathering millions in the nation's capital, they practiced and demonstrated the superpower of inclusive advocacy.

That is, gun violence is not new in America. In fact, black men account for 52 percent of all homicide victims in the United States and are ten times more likely to die at the hands of a firearm.[142] Thus, knowing the power of their platform at the time, they invited their minority peers to meet with them. They also asked them to speak and provide input at the rallies. Furthermore, they supported the causes people of color cared about.

By practicing inclusive advocacy, the #NeverAgain campaign grew, exponentially, to include survivors of gun violence regardless of race, ethnicity, sexuality, or socioeconomic status. These superheroines also began to build a bridge between the race gap and to heal racial tensions. Furthermore, they spotlighted the young – the children killed in the Sandy Hook Elementary School shooting – and the largest group impacted by mass shootings – women. With great empathy to ensure the representation of all groups impacted by gun violence, these super-heroines modeled the power of inclusive advocacy, as well as demonstrated how to make tangible steps toward change and progress.

They did not stop there. March for Our Lives traveled across the nation to most major cities, rivaling even the initial rally.[143] These advocate-activists believed that national attention to gun violence and changes in gun regulations were critical. They also believed that change would only come from engaged citizens who are registered to vote. Specifically, we need registered voters who take the threat of gun violence seriously and then vote for leaders who take gun violence seriously. Throughout their activism, they set up voter registration tables at their rallies, registering over 50,000 voters. Additionally, 800,000 voters were registered through their partnership with over 200 local mayors. According to their campaign, over forty-six NRA-backed candidates lost their elections in November 2018. There was a 47 percent increase in voter turnout for midterm elections![144]

By practicing inclusive advocacy for all who have suffered from gun violence and igniting their generation for change, they found their superpower and built their muscle of empowerment. Today, as young women, Emma, Sofie, Jacyln, and Sarah are still a powerful force for change. While they are not working together in person anymore – Sarah and Jaclyn are in college, Emma is on the road with March for Our Lives, and Sofie is working with the Florida chapter of March for Our Lives – they are still pursuing their unified goals of enacting gun reform policies[145] and electing responsive and representative government officials. Furthermore, each of them has found their own causes to support as they grow and enter the greater world of activism. From advocating for the LGBTQ+ community to joining their local student unions, each of these girls continues to give back to their communities. With this said, their most substantial contribution may be bridging the diversity divide within a common mission by practicing inclusive advocacy.

3.5.3 The Issue: Guns in America versus the World and Toxic Masculinity

We're #1! Yes, the United States of America is #1 in civilian-owned guns, #1 in mass shootings, and #1 in gun-related deaths.[146]

With only about four percent of the world's population, Americans own nearly half of the world's civilian guns.[146] In fact, no other country comes close. A distant second is Yemen – one of the world's poorest countries in the midst of a devastating civil war.[147] Furthermore, compared to other high-income countries, we also have the highest gun-related homicide and suicide rates – 25.2 times higher and 8 times higher, respectively.[148]

So why is there so much gun violence and so many mass shootings in America? Is it guns? More importantly, is there anything we can do to stop this madness?

Politicians, especially those who swear by the Second Amendment, frequently blame mass shootings on mental illness. However, data shows only

14.8 percent of mass shootings are connected with serious mental illness.[149] In fact, people with mental illness are far more likely to be victims of firearms, not the other way around. Case in point: women – not men – are more likely to suffer from mental illness, and they are the majority of victims of mass shootings. Indeed, 54 percent of mass shootings are actually domestic violence incidents.[150] And according to the Bureau of Justice Statistics, which tracks court cases involving domestic violence, 86 percent of the perpetrators of domestic violence documented in court cases are men.[151] Furthermore, a felony domestic violence conviction is the single greatest predictor of future violent crime.[152]

What is evident is that almost all mass shootings in America have one common denominator: *males* – predominantly white males.[153] So what we should be investigating and talking about is the culture of toxic masculinity and the American males who believe they should get a gun and shoot people with it.

3.6 Case Study 6: Endurance and Determination of Nada al-Ahdal Against Child Marriage, for Girls' Education

I'm not an item for sale. I'm a human being.
—Nada al-Ahdal

Endurance is an empowerment muscle that is built by practicing it over and over again. Like physical muscle, it is catapulted forward – becoming a superpower – when we face extreme challenges and overcome them victoriously. We all possess this empowerment muscle, but only a few model it, fiercely. This is because it requires we face our fears – transforming them into a powerful force for change – and, through this, discover and fortify this muscle.

One powerful model is Nada al-Ahdal (see Figure 19). Although we may feel sorry for her environment, it is her endurance over her environment that should inspire and empower us to build this muscle.

3.6.1 Herstory: How It All Began

Born and raised in Yemen, by age eleven, Nada al-Ahdal had experienced more trials and tribulations than most people will experience in their whole lifetime. While most eleven-year-old girls are playing or daydreaming about their future, Nada's future was being foiled by her parents. They wanted to sell Nada into a forced marriage, and it was only through her uncle convincing the groom that the planned nuptials were thwarted. His persuasive argument was that Nada was "too impure" for [the groom].[154] While this marriage didn't happen, her parents

Figure 19 A drawing of Nada al-Ahdal.

Source: Drawn for the Element by Gabriela Cordero Durán, used with permission.

tried again. The second time was to a twenty-six-year-old man, someone more than twice her age.[155] Having witnessed her aunt commit suicide after being abused as a child bride, Nada feared the same.

3.6.2 Solution: Social Media Spreads the Message

It was then Nada took action! She ran to her uncle, who believed in her future.

Sadly, Nada's trauma is not unique. Being treated as a commodity – goods to be sold, exchanged, and exploited – is a reality for many girls and young women worldwide. What's even sadder is that this treatment – child marriage and other cultural practices – is forced on girls by those who love them the most – their parents and family members.

And yet, Nada's story *is* unique. To start, she endured. She survived an extraordinary challenge, not once but twice. Second, she transformed her fear into a powerful call to action. Awakening to the possibility that her voice could be a megaphone for change, she chose to share her story with the world. Using social media, she filmed a passionate, heart-wrenching three-minute plea detailing the harsh reality of child marriage – crushed dreams, ruined futures, and the destruction of the human soul and spirit. In the video, she not only also described her situation but also shared the horrific story of her aunt, who set herself on fire after being forced into marriage at the age of fourteen.[156]

Taking the world by storm, paving the way for her to launch a platform as an activist, Nada's video reached more than eight million views in one month.[157] The simple language of an eleven-year-old touched the hearts and minds of people around the world. Furthermore, her call to action reignited the conversation on child marriage around the globe.

> *I would have had no life, no education. Don't they have any compassion? I am*
> *better off dead; I would rather die. Go ahead and marry me off. I will kill*
> *myself. Some children decided to throw themselves into the sea. They are*
> *dead now ... It is not (their) fault. I am not the only one. It can happen to any*
> *child. They (society, parents, etc.) have killed our dreams![158]*

Fighting for the future of all girls just like her, Nada started the Nada Foundation four years after her video. With a mission to protect children's human rights as laid out by the United Nations, the Foundation supports initiatives to end child marriage and slavery by education, safe haven shelters, and an awareness program with resources and support.[159]

With this said, Nada faced backlash and attacks for her actions – a common reaction, particularly in societies where challenging traditional practices is synonymous with challenging authority and power.

In fact, immediately following the release of her video and a petition for the bill to be passed that would prohibit marriage until the age of eighteen, Nada was arrested and detained by Yemen security forces.[160] She was accused of working for Western actors and undermining the state of Yemen. Then, less than three months later, she was interrogated for seven hours while her uncle was detained by the Yemen government.[160] This was an effort to have them sign a legal document stating they would not publicize her story or speak with the media concerning child marriage. Furthermore, two years later, Nada was placed under "house arrest" by Huthie militants with a goal of preventing her from traveling to Switzerland in order to attend a ceremony where she was being honored for her work in ending child marriage.[161] In addition to her national government, she was also unwelcomed by many in the community. Lastly, her own family betrayed her for money.[162]

But Nada endured. Forging ahead, she spoke at TEDx, through the Foundation giving eight scholarships to schools for girls to continue their educations, and writing a memoir – leading to her nomination for the Nobel Prize for Children in 2018.[163] With each action, every single accomplishment, she used her voice and the simple tool of storytelling.

3.6.3 The Issue: Child Marriage, Worldwide

Child marriage is not unique – to Nada or Yemen. According to Girls Not Brides, a global partnership committed to ending child marriage, every year, fifteen million girls are married before their eighteenth birthday.

This is one girl every two seconds.

This isn't exclusive to economically poor countries. Child marriage is legal and practiced in forty-six states of the United States.[164] In one decade – from 2000 to 2010 – nearly a quarter of a million children were married off.[164]

In Nada's home country of Yemen, 31.9 percent of girls are married before they turn eighteen.[165] Of those, around 9.4 percent are married even before fifteen despite the fact that the law states fifteen years old is the marriageable age.[165]

Sadly, the number one perpetrator of selling girls is their own parents. And the primary reason for this heinous act – a form of modern day slavery and domestic violence – is money or, more accurately, the belief of money – a better financial future for the family and the girl. Furthermore, this antiquated practice is about power: girls are worth less than boys. And the consequence of this false belief about girls and power has led to more than 700 million girls and women being married before their eighteenth birthday.[166] It is estimated that by 2030 another 150 million girls will be married before their eighteenth birthday.[166]

This is why in September 2011 the Elders, a group founded by Nelson Mandela along with Archbishop Desmond Tutu, Mary Robinson, and other global leaders, took on ending child marriage as one of their core work for peace and human rights. This became Girls Not Brides, a global partnership of more than 1,300 civil society organizations, including 4GGL, from over 100 countries – all committed to ending child marriage and enabling girls to fulfill their potential.

3.7 Case Study 7: Holistic Healing from War and Gender-Based Violence of Ukrainian Girls

Healing is when you regain your desire to live...
—Yuliya Sporysh

Healing is not the same as treating. Although healing may involve treatment, it goes beyond it, and holistically – mind, body, and soul. In fact, healing literally means "to make whole." With the same root word as health, healing is a process of "restoration to health" or "restoration of wholeness." Healing is a rare practice, particularly in the Western world. And yet, it must be the aim and the approach after traumatic events. Otherwise, as the saying goes: "Those who don't transform pain, will transmit pain."

So, how do we, in fact, bring about healing? Moreover, how do we go about it in particularly challenging circumstances like war zones where violence – particularly gender-based violence – is pervasive and perpetrated with impunity?

Ukrainian NGO Girls (or Girls) is endeavoring to do so (see Figure 20). What began as essential sexual reproductive health education has gone beyond to change gender norms and stereotypes by creating sociocultural campaigns

Figure 20 A drawing of girls behind the nongovernmental organization Girls in the Ukraine.

Source: Drawn for the Element by Gabriela Cordero Durán, used with permission.

debunking outdated mindsets and behaviors in their society. Today, they are at the forefront of the Russian invasion of Ukraine, providing vital humanitarian aid as well as holistic support and services in order to heal their country. More specifically, Girls provides mental health care – psychological and psychothera-peutic assistance critical to healing – for victims and survivors of gender-based violence, including their male family members. They realized building the empowerment muscle of healing is essential to their long-term survival.

Indeed, the Ukrainians are powerfully and courageously demonstrating to the rest of the world their resilience and determination to win the war against the Russian regime. And at the forefront are Girls practicing healing as their lives depend on it.

3.7.1 Herstory: How It All Began

Yuliya Sporysh was giving birth to her second child in a Kyiv maternity hospital when she noticed something strange about many of the young mothers-to-be. Rather than experiencing the joy and exhilaration of becoming a mother, they were sad and confused. Not having learned about sexual reproductive health, they were not just unprepared for pregnancy and childbirth but also downright terrified about what was about to happen and felt like victims waiting for doomsday.

Most of this great angst and worry stems from Ukrainian culture and society, where even today, the only role for females is to be a good wife and mother, and yet, it doesn't prepare them for motherhood with any education, beginning with sexual reproductive health education.

Therefore, to learn exactly what teen girls, their mothers, and the school staff with whom these teen girls interact know – or more accurately, do not know – about sexuality and reproductive health, Yuliya conducted a survey. The results were profound:[167]

- More than half of teen girls report that they are *not* able to have open and calm conversations with their mothers about reproductive and sexual health.
- More than half of teen girls avoid or find it difficult to talk about sexual violence, including rape.
- Teen girls find it difficult to talk to their mothers – about sexual and reproductive health – because they worry about their mothers' negative reactions to their curiosity.
- 64 percent of females believe that abortion leads to infertility.
- 60 percent believe that children should be born in marriage only.

3.7.2 Solution: Sexual Education and Access to Automobiles

Educating and empowering girls and young women is the gateway to transforming societies. They not only give birth to future generations but also shape and nurture their mindset. Thus, to shape the mindset and prepare a new reality of young mothers-to-be, Yuliya developed and organized a sexual education series called Lectures for Girls. Collaborating with a gynecologist whom she met in the maternity hospital, they began with a small group of girls.

Quickly, the educational effort grew in popularity, receiving an overwhelming number of requests from schools and parents for sexual education – for both boys and girls. In 2019, Lectures for Girls became an NGO, "Girls." And even – and especially – during the pandemic, when people could not readily get access to health care, Girls delivered essential sexual and reproductive health education. In fact, with funds from UNICEF, they were able to grow their team and scale their work. In summary, Girls provided thousands of hours of critical education in remote villages and small towns in Ukraine for more than 100,000 youth.[168] Moreover, they provided hygiene kits and trained teachers about menstrual health and hygiene across Ukraine.

As Yuliya described it, "We give the girls the inspiration, hope, and instruments to live a secure, fulfilled and engaged life. We provide them with comprehensive mental health support, reliable information about their sexual and reproductive health and rights, as well as engage with career guidance, professional development, and financial freedom. We educate, protect, engage and mentor girls during the coming-of-age period."

3.7.3 The Issue: Violence Against Girls and Women
in Warzones, Ukraine

On February 24, 2022, NGO Girls, along with every human soul in Ukraine, awoke to their greatest nightmare. The Russian regime had begun a full-scale invasion of their sovereign nation. Yuliya and her family were directly affected by the initial Russian violence as her home city was just outside of Kyiv.

However, brutal dictators and their large military force cannot stop Girl Power. As soon as Yuliya and her family were safe, she immediately began putting NGO Girls to work, again. Furthermore, now, more than ever, they focused on practicing the empowerment muscle of healing – providing holistic support and services for casualties of the war. That is, going beyond their usual sexual educational services, NGO Girls provides humanitarian aid and psychological assistance to teenagers, women, and children from large families. Furthermore, Girls provides basic and yet vital life skills to young women – like obtaining a driver's license so that they can drive away from danger or toward help, and be mobile in general. Girls knew that families have cars that are sitting unused as the men are away fighting the war. The females do not know how to drive, and those living in small villages can't get to the bigger towns or cities for things like a doctor's appointment or work.

In Yuliya's words,

> We are doing everything possible and [more] to help the children and women of Ukraine to get through this difficult period as well as possible. We have joined international assistance projects and attracted additional sponsors, which allows us to help even more effectively by delivering humanitarian aid to the most affected regions of Ukraine, organizing our IDP Shelter Center, providing psychological assistance, and offering therapy for of survivors of sexual violence.

This is because war is a breeding ground for violence. It initiates as well as amplifies violence that already exists in societies. Indeed, in war, violence is like water, spreading and permeating every fabric of life. Furthermore, endemic issues like domestic violence are perpetuated with impunity.

Case in point: the Russian attack is especially impacting the lives of Ukrainian women and girls on a level most of us cannot fathom – from increased risks of gender-based violence, sexual exploitation, and abuse to the loss of crucial livelihoods and rising poverty levels. For example, national police data reviewed by Reuters showed that registered domestic violence cases jumped 51 percent in 2023 compared with the same period in 2022.[169] And even if a domestic violence offender was convicted under Ukrainian law, the punishment is a maximum of just two years in prison or a fine between 170 and 340 hryvnia ($5-10) or a community service sentence.[169] And if this wasn't bad enough, the massive destruction from this war has further decimated services for survivors of violence, including essential health care and financial support.

This is why NGO Girls and other humanitarian efforts like UNFPA focusing on Ukrainian girls and women are vital to ensuring Ukraine's sustainability and, ultimately, their victory. From healing the girls to healing their nation, Girls has gone beyond its original action and is now determined to restore their wholeness and oneness.

4 Action: A Framework for Women's Empowerment

The term "women's empowerment" has been ubiquitously used and claimed in the twenty-first century. Nike's Dream Crazier advertisement profiles all-female Olympic athletes, narrated by Serena Williams. Coca-Cola's 5by20 declared that they have achieved and exceeded their goal of enabling five million women globally in economic empowerment by 2020. Google committed $25 million to fund organizations empowering women and girls to reach their full economic potential and thrive. These are just some of the many businesses and corporations touting that they are empowering a large part of the female population. As one academic study surmised, "Once used to describe grassroots struggles to confront and transform unjust and unequal power relations, [empowerment] has become a term used by an expansive discourse coalition of corporations, global non-governmental organizations, banks, philanthrocapitalists and development donors."[170]

And this is just in the private sector. In the public sector, government agencies to multilateral organizations have created a special unit or office dedicated to gender equality and women's empowerment. For example, in 2009 the US State Department appointed the first-ever ambassador-at-large to lead the Office of Global Women's Issues. The Office has the mandate "to promote the rights and empowerment of women and girls through US foreign policy."[171] One year later, a United Nations entity, UN Women, was created to promote gender equality and the empowerment of women and girls at the multilateral level.

So, with all these efforts to empower females, globally and locally, what is women's empowerment – exactly? More importantly, are they in fact empowering girls and women – or is it just rhetoric?

Despite how widely and pervasively it is used, the word "empowerment" does not exist in many languages. That is, the word "mother" has a direct correlation, an equivalent word in other languages. For example, in Spanish it is "la madre" and in French it is "la mère." However, "empowerment" does not.

Rather, this word is translated into or described according to what people think "empowerment" means or how it is used in the context – all from a Western perspective.

In fact, even in the field of gender equality and women's empowerment, there is no common definition or understanding of women's empowerment. Instead, from government agencies to multilateral institutions like the United Nations, as well as international organizations like CARE and the Bill and Melinda Gates Foundation, a great majority of the work being done in this space is on an issue – such as education, economic development, and violence against girls and women – and not on empowerment, per se.

How, then, do we truly begin this pioneering work of women's empowerment – in this case, specifically focusing on the younger generations for greater impact, sustainability, and justice?

4.1 Concretizing Women's Empowerment

Instead of some nebulous idea or wishful thinking, empowerment must be concretized for it to be a lived reality for girls and women. To start, we need to know what empowerment is and is not. That is, what empowerment is – a definition or a framework to strive for; what it is not – differentiating from and demystifying concepts with which it has been used synonymously.

The first, according to the World Bank:

> *Empowerment is the process of enhancing the capacity of individuals or groups to make choices and to transform those choices into desired actions and outcomes.*[172]

Another definition, a more comprehensive and holistic one, comes from a seventh-grade girl:

> *The dictionary says empowerment is the process of becoming stronger and more confident, especially in controlling one's life and claiming one's rights. I believe to do this each person must have a supportive environment where they feel safe and are surrounded by people who believe in them. I am fortunate to have both family and friends and teachers who accept me for who I am. I want all girls to feel this acceptance so they can reach their full potential.*

Here, it's understood that empowerment does not happen in a vacuum. As the African proverb notes: *It takes a village to raise a child.* And this wise seventh grader understands that empowerment – sustainable empowerment, that is – requires a village, an ecosystem, with social support, as well as physical safety. Most importantly, empowerment isn't hoarded, but in fact shared. Indeed, she wants all girls to be empowered, and it is this transcending element that makes empowerment powerful. In sum, *empowered people empower people*. In this way, empowerment is a holistic and regenerative process, training, and model for individuals to follow, and an ecosystem for sustainable change.

Another way to concretize empowerment is to differentiate it from what it is not – neither equality nor equity. Although the three words – equality, equity, and empowerment – are frequently used interchangeably, they are distinct and different.

Figure 21 is an attempt to show the differences. It shows equality as sameness – the same number of representation or amount of compensation no matter the individual differences. Equity is shown as fairness – a fair amount of compensation or treatment based on the individual needs. However, empowerment is a completely different ecosystem wherein the systemic barrier is removed, opening access to and opportunities for all. In a holistic ecosystem, individuals can become the highest, truest expression of themselves. Another way to explain this is that as opposed to the "band aid" approach to equality and equity, empowerment works to remove the barriers rather than compensate for it.

Finally, empowerment targets what's at the root – the imbalance and the domination of power. With the same root word, power and empower work, oppositely. For one, unlike power – a zero-sum game – empowerment is a win–win approach, process, and force that is restorative (i.e. restorative justice) and regenerative. Empowerment restores and heals. In turn, empowered individuals then work to empower others. In fact, it is transformed power – from domination and power over to power within, power with, and power for the collective good.

Now that we've defined empowerment, what does data tell us about women's empowerment?

Figure 21 Visualizing equality, equity, and empowerment.
Source: Author.

4.2 The First-Ever Global Data on Women's Empowerment

Gender inequality is a tenacious social virus that lives and breathes in every society in the world. Most societies have had a long – or only – history of patriarchy with sociocultural norms, practices, and policies that systemically and systematically discriminate against females.

Thus, not surprisingly, there is a dearth of data on women's empowerment. Instead, what research exists in the field is mainly focused on gender equality – or, more accurately, on *inequality*. In fact, even a long-standing gender tracker like the Global Gender Gap Report, published by the World Economic Forum, transparently states that "[their] Index ranks countries according to their proximity to gender equality rather than women's empowerment."[26]

Now, what's wrong with solely focusing on achieving gender equality, thinking that in turn, equality will bring about empowerment? That is, will gender equality result in women's empowerment? Or is it the other way around?

As noted earlier in this section, equality and empowerment are not the same. Equality is about sameness – not oneness. Furthermore, when it comes to data, it just counts and compares. That is, it counts the number of males versus females in relation to an issue, rather than understanding the lived reality of girls and women and finding out what is at the root of the disparity in order to uproot it.

For example, striving for gender equality in education has been about counting the number of boys and girls in school and comparing them. Usually, this results in a larger number of boys in school than girls, specifically in income-poor countries.

This means the gold standard is males. That is, gender equality in education means that if 90 percent of boys are in school, then the highest aspiration for girls would also be 90 percent. So rather than learning about and understanding the differences between boys and girls when it comes to education and schooling, and then striving for the greatest potential of each group, girls are relegated to settling for the level of boys' achievement.

Most importantly, focusing just on gender equality has not been sufficient, even in achieving equality. For example, it will take the United Nations – the body that envisioned, developed, and promoted the UN SDGs or global goals, which include gender equality (SDG 5) – 700 years to achieve gender parity at the level of mission directors.[173] The Global Gender Gap Report amplified this paltry reality by reporting that it will take 131 years to reach gender parity, globally, if we keep doing business as usual.[26] And this does not take into consideration unforeseeable circumstances and challenges that may stop – or even set back – progress. For example, the COVID-19 pandemic not only added more years – thirty-plus – to an already prolonged timeline, it also exacerbated existing endemics like domestic violence and financial insecurity/poverty of girls and women. If another pandemic or a crisis like war erupts, it will be centuries before humanity experiences gender parity.

Simply put, none of us will be alive to experience gender parity in our lifetime. And this is not acceptable. As Martin Luther King, Jr., famously declared, "freedom is never voluntarily given by the oppressor; it must be demanded by the oppressed." In other words, freedom – or power – is not freely given away. Actions must come from the oppressed. For girls and women, they themselves must first be empowered to lead the change. This will not only advance women's empowerment. It will also catapult gender equality forward.

So, to gather data on women's empowerment, For Girls Glocal Leadership (4GGL) collected *the first-ever* women's empowerment data, globally. (More information about the survey and the target population is in Section 2: Data.) From this data, empowerment is defined as a process of going from "I cannot" to "I can." It involves two main components: the mind (awareness) and the action. Through this process, the individual first removes mental barriers and then acts, becoming an agent of change.

Today's young women realized that they themselves are the greatest contributors to making changes in their lives. More specifically, more than 60 percent of the respondents chose self, followed by family and government as distant second and third contributors (18 percent and 15 percent, respectively).

Moreover, for those young women who became agents of change, when it came to the causality of change – that is, going from "I cannot" to "I can" – a staggering 46 percent of the respondents identified self-awareness and awakening (see Figure 22). Self-awareness was associated with knowing who they are, having self-worth and/or purpose in life, and being connected to an inner strength or a greater power source like God or nature that gives meaning in their lives.

Here are some responses in their own words: "My own awareness of things that both limit and empower me [changed my life for the better]" (Washington DC, United States). "I have become more comfortable [with my own voice] and taking the initiative to create the changes I want" (Boston, United States). "Being more aware of what I am worth has forced the change" (Trinidad).

Given that empowerment is an internal power source, it is not surprising, then, that the number one change young women seek in their lives is personal development – cultivating positive mental and spiritual skills and daily habits within themselves. These practices deepen one's understanding of who they are and their

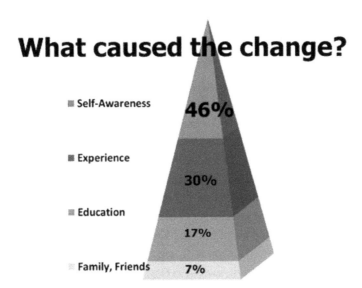

What caused the change?

- Self-Awareness — **46%**
- Experience — **30%**
- Education — **17%**
- Family, Friends — **7%**

Figure 22 Perceptions of positive change reported from a survey of young women.

Source: Author, based on the 4GGL global survey.

inherent worth and self-esteem, establishing a firm foundation from which to use their voices and take action for change. While there were some outliers in the Middle East (due to intense conflict and war, their #1 change was to leave their country for safety), aspiration for personal development and self-awareness spanned all regions, economic status and cultures, depicting a new generation of women who are actively looking for ways to grow and strengthen their muscles of empowerment, beginning with making changes in their own lives. This was followed by job/career change.

Lastly, and importantly, young women stated that women's empowerment requires a holistic system, including mentors and supportive adults, as well as a safe and secure environment. In fact, this support system is how some defined "women's empowerment" – the power of support to make women strong. And those who answered that they can make changes had a support system, the core being their families, helping them to find their voice and take action.

4.3 Three Shocking Truths about Women's Empowerment

In summary, the three big takeaways from the 4GGL global survey of young women around the world about their empowerment were:

1. Education $\neq$ Empowerment. That is, education and empowerment may show correlation, but not causation.

2. Young women in economically rich countries are not more empowered than young women in economically poor countries.
3. In fact, the key to empowerment is not external. It's internal!

These three truths are inherently and perhaps even subversively revolutionary. For one, education has been the main – and most times, the only – focus when it comes to girls' empowerment. As one academic study proclaims, "Education is ... a key factor in women's empowerment."[174] Another study parrots that "women's access to education is a critical factor in their empowerment,"[175] while a third claims that "education is the key factor for women's empowerment, prosperity, development and welfare."[176]

With this new data and knowledge from the 4GGL global survey, it is time to rethink, re-strategize, and transform the old ways of doing sustainable development. This is not to say education isn't important. Education is critical and the foundation for building civil societies. However, our data shows education alone will not bring about women's empowerment.

Another revolutionary finding from this data is that despite the goal of most countries to become economically developed to bring about social development, women's empowerment is not dependent on money. In fact, individual wealth can be a barrier to empowerment. As Figure 22 shows, the more we practice creating change – action – the better and more courageous we become. And girls and young women in poor countries get more practice, going from I cannot to I can, than those living in rich countries.

Lastly, contrary to conventional wisdom, empowerment is not external. It is internal. That is, empowerment isn't something that is given to you by an authority or government like rights, or obtained like education, job, money, and so on. Although these factors can contribute to and influence empowerment, significantly, empowerment is internal – power within or agency. This is in fact how the respondents differentiate between rights (external) and empowerment (internal). Furthermore, empowerment is the fuel to create the change we want in our world – in ourselves and for others. It begins with self-awakening and self-awareness, and they are strengthened through practice in bringing about change in one's own life or, even more powerfully, in the lives of others.

Albert Einstein defined insanity as doing the same thing over and over again, expecting different results. Let's stop insanity and empower instead. Today's young women are leading this change. From Iran to Hong Kong, they are at the frontline, fighting for justice and speaking truth to power. Furthermore, they are seeking personal development to become more self-aware, self-confident, and compassionate towards others.

With this said, adolescent girls and young women cannot do it alone. They need help and support, as well as practical tools to further their empowerment and spread it to those around them. The good news is that every single person, organization, institution, and government can take action to support girls' and young women's empowerment today. We can support girls and young women in self-actualizing their own inner power – to truly empower them.

Now more than ever, empowerment training is needed, and today's empowered girls and young women, fighting for social, economic, and political change, are demonstrating how.

Section 3 profiles seven powerful superheroines or a group of superheroines with their superpower – a muscle of empowerment. Through each case study, we can learn and build our own muscles of empowerment – inner power and tools to utilize to take action for positive change, now!

4.4 Building the Empowerment Muscle of Focus

A common theme of superheroes is that they transform their tragedy and pain into a powerful force for change. This is what Greta Thunberg has done, cultivating her superpower of focus by channeling her pain into building her empowerment muscle. And she demonstrates the focus empowerment muscle, powerfully, particularly in our attention deficit, social media noise-filled world. However, unlike fictional superhero char-acters, Greta's herstory is real. By turning her real-life experience of being bullied because of her autism into an empowerment muscle, she uses it to fight for her future, as well as everyone's future, including those who bullied her.

And Greta demonstrates focus, powerfully. She deliberately chooses direct words, poignant phrases, and concise data throughout her speeches. She is not sidetracked by politics, fame, or social pressures. Instead, she speaks truth to power – speaking directly to politicians and world leaders to tell them they have failed her generation, robbing them and subsequent generations of their childhood.

So how can we build our empowerment muscle of focus?

4.4.1 Focus Empowerment Muscle Training 101

To begin, scan your mind and memory for an issue, discrimination, or injustice – social, political, or economic in nature – you or someone you care about has experienced. If there are none, identify an issue, discrimin-ation, or injustice you've heard of that you'd like to learn more about and could support.

- Take thirty minutes to one hour to describe what happened – narrate a story.
- Investigate and research this issue. Write down impressions, key words, thoughts, and your reactions to the following:

  - Who/which group of people does this issue impact, uniquely or particularly?
  - Why does it happen? What is the root cause?
  - What actions are taken currently, if anything, to address the problem and alleviate suffering?

Mind, Body, and Spirit Scan:

- Which aspects of the issue are you most interested in and why?

  - Take five to ten minutes to focus on how your body feels as you consider the issue. If you find your mind wandering on other thoughts or tasks you need to do, make note of them and set them aside. Calmly re-center, coming back to the issue at hand. It may be helpful to use key words in your writing to help restore and regain focus.
  - Write down everything about the issue that is clear to you and that you feel strongly about. Notice how your body feels as you write them.
  - Write down everything that is unclear or unfocused in your mind. Notice how your body feels as you write them.
  - Now, take time each day to focus on what you feel strongly about, and how your inner body reacts.

Action Steps:

  - After you've gained a sense of clarity and focus for the issue and story, write down all the possible things – big and small – you can do.
  - Scan your family, school, and community for support, resources, and partnership.
  - Pick one action you can do and begin the change, now.
  - Before *and* after each time you take action, take three to five minutes to restore and regain your focus on the issue at hand – the greater goal – particularly if you get fixated on a side issue or a problem you've run into.

4.5 Building the Empowerment Muscle of Solidarity

When we envision empowerment in the West, the image that most likely comes into our mind is an individual athlete, politician, or CEO of a company. This is because Western culture is highly individualistic – and individual self is at the center and the focus, as well as the outcome. The members of such societies are hardwired to see empowerment as one leader, one heroine.

However, there are collective societies around the world whose members believe in and practice collectivism – common interest and mutual support – automatically. Here, solidarity is the source *and* the outcome of the empowerment muscle. And this kind of power not only fuels but also sustains for the long term.

Solidarity, as a vital component of empowerment, is also confirmed by our data collected from the 4GGL Young Women's Empowerment global survey. It showed that true empowerment isn't possible if it isn't for everyone – inclusive. Therefore, the aim must be for the whole group – to restore power to the whole marginalized community. This again reiterates: *empowered people empower people.*

Therefore, solidarity is vital to people's power and movement building. And the Hong Kong protest is a powerful example in the twenty-first-century with these ninja warriors as twenty-first century's justice warriors. They – Hong Kong's adolescent girls and young women – are at the frontline fighting a major geopolitical power – China, which even nations fear; they are the superheroes of our time, redefining what girls and women can do – and have been doing – as well as how they can bring about powerful change in the world.

The element of collectivism is what makes this empowerment muscle exceptional. That is, these changemakers aren't just fighting for themselves. More importantly, they are making the sacrifice for the greater good – their nation's freedom. Furthermore, their action is not for individual glory or recognition. Instead, their unified goal is to generate a ripple effect within the whole city-state to fight for democracy.

The Girl Power of the Hong Kong protest and their practice of the solidarity empowerment muscle their fellow freedom fighters is a particularly powerful model in today's highly individualistic, divisive world. While many nations are inflamed by partisanship, the internal civil war of political parties, the Hongkongers – young and old, rich and poor, females and males – are united. They are unified in solidarity in their fight for democracy where the voices of their people – not China – will govern its nation.[177]

With this said, solidarity does not mean conformity. Instead, it acknowledges and embraces our differences, and yet simultaneously sees we are more powerful together. In fact, it is indeed our differences that fill the gaps and complement one another, in the pursuit of one goal. We are not the same, nor should we strive to be similar. And yet, as human beings, we all seek the same things – freedom, liberty, and happiness – as well as experience challenges and setbacks.

4.5.1 Solidarity Empowerment Muscle Training 101

To begin, scan your mind and your memory bank for an issue, discrimination, or injustice – social, political, or economic in nature – you or someone you care about has experienced. If there are none, search for or research a social injustice or inequity issue you can take a stand in solidarity with others.

- Take thirty minutes to one hour to describe the story.
- Investigate and research this issue. Write down impressions, key words, thoughts, and your reactions to the following:

  - Who/which group of people does this issue impact, uniquely or particularly?
  - Why does it happen? What is the root cause?
  - What actions are being taken currently, if anything, to address the problem and alleviate suffering?

Mind, Body, and Spirit Scan:

- Can you empathize with this issue?
- Take five to ten minutes to focus on how your body feels as you consider the issue.
- Write down everything about the issue that is clear to you and that you feel strongly about. Notice how your body feels as you write them.
- Write down everything that is unclear or unfocused in your mind. Notice how your body feels as you write them.
- Now, take time each day to focus on what you feel strongly about, and how your inner body reacts.

Action Steps:

- Research and identify several groups or organizations that are taking action – big and small – in addressing the issue.
- Pick one group to join in solidarity and begin the change, now.
- Scan your family, school, and community for support, resources, and partnership in your solidarity empowerment muscle building.

4.6 Building the Empowerment Muscle of Hope

Many of us may practice hope on a regular basis. For instance, we hope it won't rain. We hope for safe travel.

With this said, Fatemah hopes on a scale and magnitude most of us can't imagine. She embodies a new generation of Afghan women who no longer accept the status quo, inequities, and domination of power by one group. Instead, she actively hopes for and envisions a brighter future. Then, she acts toward that vision.

Though your obstacles may not look like hers – poverty, gender discrimination, terrorism, attack on your hometown, and the death of your father at the hands of an international terrorist group – they are perfect for building your muscle of empowerment.

Fatemah's hope did not stem from her ability to overcome the obstacles in her life. Rather, she hopes despite the unknown. This hope comes from an inner source or a spiritual source which enables her to believe that a better, brighter future exists. Her hope is a superpower and an empowerment muscle, one that, like any other, requires constant stretching and use to maintain and strengthen it. As she worked toward and realigned her vision, she never lost sight of the end goal – the goal to provide access to STEM education for girls across Afghanistan. Hope enabled her to face the obstacles head-on and fight another day. It strengthened her voice and choice and helped empower others along her journey – a journey that, like yours, is an ongoing process.

4.6.1 Hope Empowerment Muscle Training 101

To begin, scan your mind and memory for an issue, discrimination, or injustice – social, political, or economic in nature – for which you hope for a better future. If there are none, search for or research about a social injustice or inequity that you'd like to support.

- Take thirty minutes to one hour to describe the story.
- Investigate and research this issue. Write down impressions, key words, thoughts, and your reactions to the following:

  - Who/which group of people does this issue impact, uniquely or particularly?
  - Why does it happen? What is the root cause?
  - What actions are taken currently, if anything, to address the problem and alleviate suffering?

Mind, Body, and Spirit Scan:

- What gives you hope about this issue? Write down your thoughts and feelings.
- Take some time to visualize a better future for this issue. Write down one to three things that can get better – things that you *hope* for. Visualize the future

while holding on to your hope, for at least a few minutes, but as long as necessary to feel and/or believe it is possible.

- Continue to sit with your visualization of a better future, holding the moment and space with hope filling your inner awareness.
- Take five to ten minutes to focus on how your body feels as you consider the issue.
- Write down everything about the issue that is clear to you and that you feel strongly about. Notice how your body feels as you write them.
- Write down everything that is unclear or unfocused in your mind. Notice how your body feels as you write them.
- Take time each day to focus on what you feel strongly about and how your inner body reacts.

Action Steps:

- After you've gained a sense of clarity on the issue and the desired outcome you hope for, research organizations or groups that are working toward the same goal.
- Contact them, beginning with two to three of them first if you've found many.
- Pick one you're most interested in working with and begin the change, now.
- Scan your family, school, and community for support, resources, and partnership.

4.7 Building the Empowerment Muscle of Courage

Courage may be an empowerment muscle we think we will never need to practice. And yet, it is a vital empowerment muscle for making our world better.

For the Chibok girls, long before the abduction, they were practicing courage, daily. The town of Chibok is a patriarchal society with very few choices and opportunities for girls and young women to thrive. Furthermore, due to its proximity to the Boko Haram territory, girls who were getting an education beyond the primary level took great risk – risk so high that armed guards and gates surrounded them for protection.

However, like Fatemah with her empowerment muscle of hope, the Chibok girls also believed that education was worth the risk because it can change their current circumstances to a better life. They built their empowerment muscle of courage, regularly, as they grappled with the reality that their life trajectory was grim, and that they needed to fight for their right to education.

Yes, the courage muscle is built through continual trials rather than a few abysmal encounters. It is formed and strengthened with each obstacle, and for these girls, it began even before they were born.

While today many of the Chibok girls have been reunited with their community and families, they still face the obstacle of reintegration. Sadly, the threat presented by Boko Haram has led to strong distrust across Nigeria for all those directly impacted by their actions. From their families believing they are now loyal to Boko Haram or military officials treating them as terrorists, their lives are still in danger and faced by uncertainty.

None of these circumstances can negate their superpower of courage and its impact on the world around them. In the face of adversity with options that are rife with uncertainty and fear, they persevered and continue to do so. They tell their stories and rebuild their lives. In doing so, they lift each other up and create a community for themselves and those who come after them. Furthermore, practicing their superpower of courage does not mean their lives are now perfect – the picture of empowerment from a Western lens. On the contrary, the Chibok girls model courage and vulnerability providing an example for all of us to use to create real change in our world.

4.7.1 Courage Empowerment Muscle Training 101

What does courage mean to you? In order to do so, you may need to first ask yourself: what are you afraid of? Why?

Now, name one current issue, discrimination, or injustice – social, political, or economic in nature – that resonates with you.

- Take thirty minutes to one hour to describe the issue.
- Investigate and research this issue. Write down impressions, key words, thoughts, and your reactions to the following:

  - Who/which group of people does this issue impact, uniquely or particularly?
  - Why does it happen? What is the root cause?
  - What actions are taken currently, if anything, to address the problem and alleviate suffering?

Mind, Body, and Spirit Scan:

- Focusing on your heart, write down what you feel about this issue.
- Take five to ten minutes to focus on how your body feels as you consider the issue.
- Write down everything about the issue that is clear to you and that you feel strongly about. Notice how your body feels as you write them.
- Write down everything that is unclear or unfocused in your mind. Notice how your body feels as you write them.

- Take time each day to focus on what you feel strongly about and how your inner body reacts.

Action Steps:

- After you've gained a sense of clarity for the issue, research organizations or groups that are working toward the same goal.
- Do you believe courage is needed to take bold action with the organization you've identified? Explain why or why not.
- Contact the organization and begin the change, now.
- Scan your family, school, and community for support, resources, and partnership in this service.

4.8 Building the Empowerment Muscle of Advocacy

Advocacy is born from a deep desire for change, not only for oneself but particularly for others. Although we may not experience a life-altering tragedy, like a school shooting, every single one of us will face challenges that we can use to build the empowerment muscle of advocacy.

And finding our inner advocacy requires opening ourselves to our pain and transcending it to have empathy for others. It can also include anger – anger at the world for the current state of affairs.

This is exactly what Emma, Sarah, Sofie, and Jaclyn did. Channeling their grief, pain, and anger at adults for failing to protect them, they galvanized their community for positive change for all gun violence victims. They lifted up others, showing them that their voices matter and amplifying their voices, along with their own. They raised their voices in unison.[178]

> *[A]lthough to some, we may seem fully capable of running this revolution on our own. We need you. My generation is an agent of change, and we are proud of that. But adults should not feel excused from taking action – the pressure we are under is real. We are teenagers with the weight of the country on our shoulders. We absolutely need your support.[179]*

4.8.1 Advocacy Empowerment Muscle Training 101

Advocacy is about public support, particularly for a policy or a policy change. Thus, think about and reflect on social discrimination or an injustice that you'd like to take action on to change policy. If there is none, search for or research policies that perpetuate social injustice or inequity.

- Take thirty minutes to one hour to describe the issue.

- Investigate and research this issue. Write down impressions, key words, thoughts, and your reactions to the following:

  - Who/which group of people does this issue impact, uniquely or particularly?
  - Why does it happen? What is the root cause?
  - What actions are taken currently, if anything, to address the problem and alleviate suffering?

Mind, Body, and Spirit Scan:

- Which aspects of the issue are you most interested in and why?
- Take five to ten minutes to focus on how your body feels as you consider the issue.
- Write down everything about the issue that is clear to you and that you feel strongly about. Notice how your body feels as you write them.
- Write down everything that is unclear or unfocused in your mind. Notice how your body feels as you write them.
- Take time each day to focus on what you feel strongly about, and how your inner body reacts to sitting with clarity and focus.

Action Steps:

- After you've gained a sense of clarity about the issue, search several (three) policy organizations that work on this issue.
- One by one, contact them requesting an interview to learn more about the issue, their policy stand, and action.
- Pick one organization's policy and begin the change, now.
- Scan your family, school, and community for support, resources, and partnership.

4.9 Building the Empowerment Muscle of Endurance

Endurance is a muscle of empowerment that every one of us can build and utilize at any time in our lives. However, it requires continuous or prolonged adversity, struggles, and challenges to strengthen it.

This is exactly what Nada did. Not only did she learn to build the empowerment muscle of endurance, she also made it into her superpower, using it and showing others – just like her, particularly in Yemen – how they too can build this empowerment muscle.

Although most of us in the Western world may only associate endurance with sports champions, girls and young women like Nada al-Ahdal who live in a war zone, refugee camp, ghetto, or in poverty practice this empowerment muscle every single day.

This means we shouldn't avoid challenges. In fact, the moment we face an obstacle is the moment our endurance empowerment muscle can begin its first curl upwards. However, this begins with a shift of our mindset – from "I cannot" to "I can!" and from "I'm not enough" to "I am enough." Then, move forward no matter what comes our way, flexing our empowerment muscle of endurance.

4.9.1 Endurance Empowerment Muscle Training 101

Like physical muscle training, endurance empowerment muscle building is long-term energy for inner strength. This mean you must identify where you might be stuck and face the challenges or barriers.

- Take thirty minutes to one hour to describe the challenge or barrier to progress.
- Research and reflect on what is at the core of the challenge or barrier.

Mind, Body, and Spirit Scan:

- Take five to ten minutes to focus on how your body feels as you reflect on your challenge.
- Write down everything that is clear to you about the challenge. Notice how your body feels as you write them.
- Write down everything that is unclear to you. Notice how your body feels as you write them.
- Take time each day to focus on what you feel strongly about, and how your inner body reacts.

Action Steps:

- Scan your family, school, and community for help and support to face your obstacle(s).
- Search for and research ways others have overcome the challenges or barriers you've identified.
- Search for or research communities or groups to join in your effort to build your endurance empowerment muscle.

4.10 Building the Empowerment Muscle of Healing

In Western culture, healing is mainly associated with medical care. And in this space, it's mostly about prescriptive medicine – man-made chemicals – to treat symptoms and to mitigate pain. In Eastern and traditional cultures, healing is a process, approached holistically to restore integrity and wholeness. This requires care and services for not just the physical body but also the mind, the heart, and the soul.

Healing is needed everywhere. In war zones, healing is the essential ingredient for the sustainability of a country and society, and women's empowerment is key. Therefore, on October 31, 2000, the United Nations Security Council adopted a resolution on women and peace and security (UNSCR 1325) with four pillars (see Figure 23).[180]

Indeed, evidence shows that higher levels of gender equality are directly related to increased levels of security and stability, key parts of the healing process, and women's participation increases the probability of a peace agreement lasting at least two years by 20 percent and a peace agreement lasting fifteen years by 35 percent.[181] Yet despite these powerful facts about healing and peace, girls and women are excluded from decision-making for both. Unconscionably, they are used as a weapon of war.

Instead of being dehumanized as weapons, or becoming part of the cycle of violence itself, healing offers a fundamentally different pathway. Indeed, the

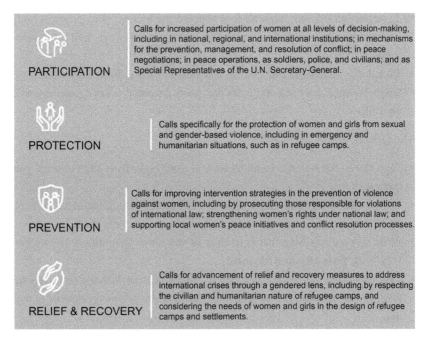

PARTICIPATION Calls for increased participation of women at all levels of decision-making, including in national, regional, and international institutions; in mechanisms for the prevention, management, and resolution of conflict; in peace negotiations; in peace operations, as soldiers, police, and civilians; and as Special Representatives of the U.N. Secretary-General.

PROTECTION Calls specifically for the protection of women and girls from sexual and gender-based violence, including in emergency and humanitarian situations, such as in refugee camps.

PREVENTION Calls for improving intervention strategies in the prevention of violence against women, including by prosecuting those responsible for violations of international law; strengthening women's rights under national law; and supporting local women's peace initiatives and conflict resolution processes.

RELIEF & RECOVERY Calls for advancement of relief and recovery measures to address international crises through a gendered lens, including by respecting the civilian and humanitarian nature of refugee camps, and considering the needs of women and girls in the design of refugee camps and settlements.

Figure 23 Four pillars of enhancing peace and security for women.
Source: [180]

founder of NGO Girls, Yuliya Sporysh, poignantly stated, "Healing is when you regain your desire to live." Girls knows the power of healing. Building the empowerment muscle of healing for oneself, as well as for others, is essential to Ukrainian survival after the Russian attack.

Although we may not be in a war zone, it is just as critical for every one of us to build our own muscle of healing. We have all experienced pain – physical, mental, or emotional. Many of us have also faced great trauma or tragedy. All require deep reflection, forgiveness, and grace.

With this said, this Element does not attempt to be an expert on healing. Healing is an art, a profession, and a way of life with long-standing wisdom that has been gathered through mindful practices. We encourage everyone to begin building this empowerment muscle – no matter where you are in life.

4.10.1 Healing Empowerment Muscle Training 101

Healing is a holistic process to restore to wholeness, oneness. The healing empowerment muscle can build strength and resilience for all other empowerment muscles. Four core aspects of healing to consider are: the physical body, the mental mind including emotions, the spiritual being, and the social support community.

- To begin this training, scan all four aspects one by one: your physical body, your mental state including emotions, your spiritual state, and your social support.
- Take thirty minutes to one hour to describe and write down each aspect.
- Scan your memory bank and write down any trauma you have experienced in your life.

Mind, Body, and Spirit Scan:

- Take five to ten minutes to focus on how your body feels as you recall your trauma(s).
- Write down everything that is clear to you and any strong feelings that come up for you, now. Notice how your body feels as you write them.
- Write down everything that is unclear to you about the trauma. Notice how your body feels as you write them.
- Take time each day to be conscious of and be present with the emotions and feelings that arise when you reflect on the trauma you've experienced in your life.

Action Steps:

- Identify a family member, a trusted friend, or another trusted adult to share how you feel. Schedule a time to share with them.

- If you have a deep wound, consider receiving mental health support.
- Search for a community service group – related to your trauma or not – that you can serve and support.

4.11 Building Empowerment Muscles and a Framework for Action

Now that you have read and reflected on these seven powerful stories with their empowerment muscles, hopefully you are getting a sense of what empowerment muscles are and how building these muscles can help you change your world. The muscle building can begin one muscle at a time, much like an athlete toning and strengthening a single part of their body. However, empowerment is a holistic exercise for the whole body. Using and flexing these muscles is more powerful when two or more are being exercised together. In fact, the transformative potential of empowerment is best attained by flexing all seven muscles in concert as an integrative training (see Figure 24).

Flexing these muscles in unison can enable the exerciser to become more empowered. Moreover, they can also have direct policy implications for achieving the empowerment of others. *Empowered people empower people.*

Figure 24 The seven muscles of empowerment as a holistic regimen.
Source: Author.

With this said, although the concept of "female empowerment" has been widely recognized by the United Nations, global development organizations, and even corporations as a fundamental step on the path toward sustainable global development since the 1980s, it also risks becoming a buzzword, used and repeated so often that its true intention and meaning are diluted. The original goals of female empowerment were big and bold – to transform gender inequality, break down societal structures that oppress women, and mobilize women politically – but today programs tend to be much narrower. Instead of addressing the root causes of gender oppression and subordination, many female empowerment initiatives are more tokenistic and limited in scope, such as those that send livestock or microloans to women in developing countries.

Embracing multidimensional empowerment, and targeting the next generation of practitioners, activists, and policymakers, can begin with our educational institutions. It can start in high school and up, in formal and informal education. But broader structural reforms are needed as well. Ending all forms of discrimination against girls and women is vital for inclusive sustainable development. Yet, today in the twenty-first century, 150 countries still have laws that treat females and males differently[182] – for example, making it difficult for women to own property, open bank accounts, start businesses, and enter certain professions. Other systemic, soul-crushing, and gender-destructive forms of oppression that need dismantling are glass ceilings and pay disparities; legal gender-based discrimination, which exists in 155 countries (see Figure 25); a lack of political representation; systemic gender-based violence, the patriarchy, and misogyny; cultural norms that exacerbate gender inequality, such as child marriage and FGM; sex-selective abortions and son-preferences; and obstacles to self-determination and the inability to make their own health care decisions.

Empowerment is about power – as in the word itself. Thus, to empower is to restore power to those whose power was taken away. For policymakers, this means examining and reviewing existing policies at every level – individual, community, national, and international. But first, they themselves must see girls and young women as *agents of change, not victims to save*. This is critical today as large swaths of sub-Saharan Africa and many countries around the world have a large youth population. Girls (and youth, for that matter) must be included in domestic and foreign policy.

Furthermore, one-off economic gifts may benefit individuals for a limited amount of time, but we need a much more expansive view of female empowerment in order to improve gender equality around the world. This entails dismantling the cultural and societal obstacles that keep women and girls subjugated and inferior.

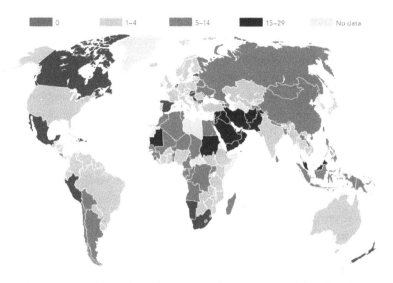

Figure 25 Number of employment and entrepreneurship-related laws differentiating between women and men.

Source: [183]

In fact, now there is indisputable data showing girls' empowerment is the most powerful force for achieving the SDGs. However, this requires a fundamental change in the mindset of power holders, which is precisely the goal of this Element – literally to show Girl Power. Langer and colleagues offer four inspiring suggestions for enhancing empowerment in the domain of gender and health that are easily adaptable for harnessing female empowerment for the achievement of the SDGs as a whole.[94] These are to:

1. *Value and prioritize girls.* Ensure that access to education, finance, health care, and other social benefits is freely available to women and girls. Put the maximum use of government resources toward achieving the availability, accessibility, and quality of government services required to address the comprehensive needs of girls.
2. *Compensate girls and women for invisible contributions to society.* Estimate the often hidden value of unpaid contributions to health care, community well-being, domestic stability, and sustainability and find ways to compensate women's invisible contributions to healthy, vibrant, functioning societies. Also seek to eliminate the gender pay gap and ensure that men and women receive equal compensation for equal work.
3. *Count women and girls in data collection and research.* Ensure that women and especially girls are accounted for in statistics and other indices of

quantification that help steer economic and financial decisions. Guarantee that sex- and age-disaggregated civil, demographic, and health statistics and survey data are obtained through national systems. Mandate that research studies enroll women and publish findings disaggregated by sex.

4. *Be accountable to women and girls.* Begin to develop and implement an accountability framework and indicators for girls and to establish independent mechanisms at global and country levels to ensure accountability for global, regional, and national action.

With all this said, not one person needs to wait for policymakers or planners at the United Nations. In fact, as you read in the seven stories, today's girls and young women are not. Any one of us can begin the process of empowerment using the framework of Self, Others, and Action.

1. Self: Build your knowledge base, learning, and understanding in depth the issue for which you are advocating.
2. Others: Find and join groups and communities with missions and values that are aligned with yours.
3. Action: Focusing on service, take action that will make your world – and thereby the greater world – better.

In fact, the history of social movements and civil disobedience suggests that a threshold for social transformation may not be as high as one thinks. Chenoweth and Stephan compellingly argue that nonviolent action via social movements and protests is twice as likely to succeed than armed conflicts and violence, and that those engaging a threshold of 3.5 percent of the population have never failed to bring about change.[184] Even if only one in ten girls and women takes the leap toward empowerment, the effect on social fabrics would be profound.

5 Conclusion: Towards a Transformative Future

As Victor Hugo wrote, "nothing else in the world . . . not all the armies . . . is so powerful as an idea whose time has come."[185] This powerful phenomenon of an idea coming to life is manifesting now. Girls and young women across the globe are empowering themselves to create, connect, and collaborate in bringing about profound transformation in their communities. And data resoundingly shows that girls' and young women's empowerment is a – and maybe the most – powerful force for changing the world.

And yet, even in the twenty-first century, whether in Sweden or Afghanistan, girls and young women live in cultures where the patriarchal mindset still persists, with norms and attitudes that perpetuate – or complicit in – gender inequality and inequity. In fact, not one country has achieved gender parity. Furthermore, less than one percent of females live in countries with both high levels of women's empowerment and high gender parity. Even more shameful is the fact that the vast majority of the world's girls and women (90 percent) are in countries where women's empowerment is dismal and a large gender gap exists.[186]

5.1 What COVID-19 (Should Have) Taught Us

In peacetime, most of us may not be thinking about gender injustice. Moreover, particularly in economically rich countries, many of us may be misguided and misinformed into thinking that the sexes are equal.

Therefore, a crisis is a wake-up call. Indeed, in times of crisis, like a pandemic or war, inequities and injustices are magnified, and an endemic like domestic violence (all forms of gender-based violence, for that matter) becomes an abscess where toxicity and other kinds of violence fester.

So, what did COVID-19 teach us?

COVID-19 and Mother Nature broadcasted for the world to see the inequities we, humans, have created and been complicit in. For one, industries hardest hit by the pandemic – like hospitality, domestic care, and service – had a female-majority work force. Second, even though women were the majority of the frontline health care workers who fought COVID-19 – 70 percent globally, 77 percent in the US[186] – only 25 percent of this sector's senior leadership was female.[186] This means the existing pay gap and other economic inequities created by our gendered industries were exacerbated during the pandemic.

COVID-19 also taught us that a lockdown, *safely*, is a privilege – and one mainly for males. That is, no matter the political system or the economic status, every single country saw domestic violence soar as girls and women were forced to shelter in place with their abusers.

In fact, the term *shadow pandemic* was coined, meaning another pandemic within the COVID pandemic. We do not know the extent of the domestic violence cases because they are generally underreported. Moreover, when education stopped abruptly, it compounded this shadow pandemic. It has been estimated that around 743 million girls were out of school during the lockdowns.[177] It can be inferred that teen pregnancies, child marriage, sex slavery, and other social illnesses that females uniquely face were also compounded. Therefore, UN Women launched the Shadow Pandemic Campaign to sound the alarm and raise awareness about the global escalation of domestic violence within the COVID-19 crisis.[187]

Lastly, and on a high note, COVID-19 taught our world a profound lesson about power. At the national level, female leaders demonstrated power differently. Indeed, "What Do Countries with the Best Coronavirus Responses Have in Common? Women Leaders."[188] From Germany's Chancellor Angela Merkel to New Zealand's Prime Minister Jacinda Ardern to Taiwan's President Tsai Ing-wen, they all flexed their empowered muscles. That is, they all practiced and demonstrated competencies – like empathy, communication, collaboration, and self-sacrificing – that are essential in a crisis as well as in today's leadership no matter if there's a crisis or not.

So why have women leaders been more successful during this pandemic?

Experts have analyzed different countries' responses to COVID-19 from the beginning, and there are several key reasons why. First, female leaders are more likely to have "inclusive political institutions."[189] That is, in these countries, the government makes decisions based on a wide array of experiences and expertise, not just a few.

A powerful example is Germany and Chancellor Merkel, which Amanda Taub's *New York Times* examination laid out: "Ms. Merkel's government considered a variety of different information sources in developing its coronavirus policy, including epidemiological models; data from medical providers; and evidence from South Korea's successful program of testing and isolation."[189]

Just by looking at a wide variety of available information, Mrs. Merkel and her government were able to limit the spread of the virus and minimize deaths relative to their neighbors.

Another reason for women leaders' success in this pandemic is their non-traditional leadership style. Traditional masculinity has been *the* political leadership style in history – literally "his-story." Yet, in a pandemic, feminine strengths, like empathy, compassion, and prevention, have worked better. By emphasizing long-term preventive measures like mask wearing and sheltering in place, female leaders have been able to decrease COVID-19 cases *and* deaths.

Taub notes a specific example of feminine leadership: "Ms. Ardern addressed the nation via a casual Facebook Live session she conducted on her phone after putting her toddler to bed. Dressed in a cozy-looking sweatshirt, she empathized with citizens' anxieties and offered apologies to anyone who was startled or alarmed by the emergency alert that announced the lockdown order."[189]

This can be contrasted with machismo male leaders who have associated masks with weakness. As a result, their countries have failed miserably, experiencing some of the highest number of cases and deaths from COVID-19 – even in the richest nation on earth, the United States of America. Indeed, COVID-19 has shown just how *toxic* toxic masculinity truly is – on families, communities, nations, and the whole world.

5.2 Call to Action: Girls and Women Changing Our World

The gender injustice and inequity exposed by COVID-19 are not new. For girls and women, it's a long list, including lack of education, wage gaps, child marriage, teen pregnancy, sex trafficking, all forms of gender-based violence, and many more.

As societies and individuals, every one of us has a hand in creating, prolonging, or ignoring these inequities and injustices. Rather than doing the hard work of digging deep and treating what is at the root of the disease – power imbalance – we keep doing the same thing, addressing just the symptoms.

As patriarchy still reigns and unfortunately, nations face the consequences of failed leadership, girls and young women around the world – like the ones in this Element! – are taking powerful actions. During the pandemic, young women like the Afghan Dreamers made a ground-breaking, low-cost ventilator from old Toyota parts using MIT's design.[190] In one of the world's poorest countries, Afghanistan, these young women produced ventilators at $500 as opposed to the usual $30,000, which was a gamechanger in the fight against COVID-19.[190]

Greta Thunberg donated $100,000 to UNICEF to support and care for children worldwide who have been affected by the COVID-19 pandemic.[191] In addition to her UNICEF donation, she won $1.5 million from the Gulbenkian Prize for Humanity, which she has pledged to donate to environmental causes affected by COVID-19.[192]

Although the pandemic may in our rearview mirror, gender-based violence and injustice persist. And in war zones like Ukraine, they are spreading like wildfire.

Thus, now is the time for each and every one of us to take action. The actions of empowered girls and young women around the world should inspire us to build and strengthen our own muscles of empowerment, not only for the $160 trillion expected to be lost due to the gender pay gap. Foremost, empowering girls and women is a moral imperative, treating them with respect, equality, and dignity. However, this new power doesn't stay and can't be hoarded by any one individual. Indeed, Girl Power is shared power, collective power, and what may well be our most powerful force for transforming the world.

6 Epilogue: Author's Herstory

6.1 A Journey of Empowerment

Freedom is not free. These words jump out at me, ironically, on the bathroom wall of the Demilitarized Zone (DMZ) between North and South Korea – where the threshold of freedom can be felt most palpably. The words continued to echo in my mind, and a few days later, I understood why. My own freedom was not inherently free. It had come at a high cost – the death of my father and an extraordinary sacrifice by my mother.

I am a girl who was born in one of the poorest countries on the globe. Like most girls living in economically poor nations, gender inequality was the norm. I experienced it early – as a seven-month-old baby – when my father died, suddenly and without a will. Sadly, fatherless baby girls had no value in the society I was born. In fact, many baby girls were discarded, sold, or neglected to die.

However, this wasn't my destiny, nor was poverty the destiny of my birth country. Coined as an "Asian Tiger" (along with Taiwan, Hong Kong, and Singapore), South Korea became a rare example of a nation that skyrocketed in economic growth and development in one generation. This was my generation. In my lifetime, I saw my birth country go from one of the poorest to the world's eleventh largest economy.

6.2 North Korea or BTS

Another way to see this extraordinary miracle is that – although unfathomable to most non-Koreans – North and South Koreas were more similar than not. Yes, *North Korea* – the darkest place on the planet with a soulless regime that does not value human life or dignity. A tale of two countries could have been the same . . . and mine. But providentially, I was born just thirty miles south of the DMZ, in Seoul, South Korea, *and* just when the two countries' destinies began to diverge. In the next two decades, the South leapfrogged the North by investing in human capital and partnering with democratic societies – specific-ally, the United States of America. Today, South Korea is the home of tech giants like Samsung and cultural pop sensations like BTS – a powerhouse and a major player in the global economy and pop culture.

With this said, the mindset of a society is tenacious. While the technology and economy of South Korea skyrocketed, its mentality, attitudes, and norms remained stuck in the old patriarchal system. The worth of females was solely connected to the status of the males in their lives. Thus, fatherless children were brutally ostracized and bullied. Consequently, fatherless girls faced double jeopardy – a sexist system and a hopeless future.

Without hope, my mother courageously left the only world she knew for a better life for us on the other side of the globe – the United States of America. Yet, this daunting endeavor came at a heart-wrenching price. My older sister and I could not go with her. In a foreign country with a language she didn't speak, no job training or work experience, *and* no social support, it would be extremely hard for her to take care of us there. So her parents made the decision for her – leave us behind, temporarily, with them while she goes alone to work tirelessly to reunite us in our new country.

The irony is that I was in fact born into a wealthy family. Only as an adult did I learn that my father's family was one of a handful of landowners of South Korea. But wealth, worth, and power were exclusively for males. My societal wealth and worth – power – ended the moment my father died.

And yet, that was exactly when my empowerment journey began. I was free to be who I truly am, not just my father's daughter. This freedom came at a great cost, and this was what I realized when I saw the sign "Freedom is not free" at the DMZ.

6.3 Coincidence or Co-incidence?

As a math major in college, I learned that coincidence is when two mathematical phenomena with no apparent relationship come together – perfectly. Coincidences, I believe, also happen in our lives.

My birth year perfectly coincides with the women's liberation movement in the United States. Across America, women were raising their voices for equal rights and freedom. As a result, Title IX passed, a federal law that prohibits sex discrimination in federally funded education programs and activities. Also in the landmark decision of *Roe* v. *Wade*, the Supreme Court held up a woman's right to choose abortion without excessive government restriction. Furthermore, the first-ever women's health and sexuality book written by and for women, *Our Bodies, Ourselves*, unleashed a movement.

This is the fertile soil on which I landed. The date was December 5, 1980. As I ran off the plane, a new reality began, starting with what should have been one of the greatest traumas in my life – the death of my father. I was just seven months old when my father passed away unexpectedly. Given I was a baby, my family created a make-believe world where *both* my mother and father immigrated to America to work hard in order to reunite us. It was only then – running into the arms of my mother only – that I learned that my father was no longer living.

Although my father's death should have been a great loss, it didn't faze me. In fact, in my new world – Texas! – I *gained* an extraordinary human being into my life. Her name was Barbara Crocker and I remember the day I found her and declared her my life's mentor. It was a beautiful summer Sunday. I was wandering around, alone, on the grounds of the church my mother attended. The church was owned by white church members who rented out space to ethnic minorities – in this case, Koreans – when it was not in use. I was alone because the older kids were at the church summer camp that I was too young to join as an eight-year-old.

When it came to church and Christianity, I didn't know much. In South Korea, where I was born and raised, most people around me were Buddhists. So when I wandered into a classroom and found a Sunday school teacher sitting alone, I took the opportunity to ask all the questions I ever had about Christianity, the Bible, and God – which were a lot!

Barbara first calmly asked me, "Are you lost? Where are you supposed to be?" I told her I was waiting for my mom who was attending the "big church." Then she did something magical – what I later learned was "southern charm." She had the gift of putting people at ease, making them feel welcome and comfortable.

Now, with genuine open-heartedness rather than cynicism or criticism, I put forth the questions I had about Christianity as it was so foreign to me. Never having heard or known of the Bible, the book seemed like a fairy-tale to me, and given she was a Sunday school teacher, I believed she must have all the answers.

However, it wasn't her answers that impressed me. It was in fact what she didn't know and how she approached the unknown that was truly transformative and empowering. First, she didn't belittle me – a girl. She also didn't give the standard answer, or what I've heard many Christians say, "That's what the Bible says." Instead, she honestly and genuinely responded to the best of her know-ledge. "I don't have all the answers, so let's go find out!" Then she gently took my eight-year-old hand and walked with me to the church bookstore, where she bought me a Bible.

Then and there began my training on the search for truth. Whenever I'd have a question for which Barbara did not have an answer, with her southern charm, she would invite me to go on a search for truth: "let's go find out!" This kind of transparent, wisdom-seeking leadership practice is just one of many reasons why I wanted Barbara to be my mentor.

Mentor in Greek means wise. And indeed, Barbara embodied wisdom that I aspired to. For example, she honored the Eastern philosophy and cultural practices that I was raised with – like "your word is your honor," collective good, and collective rising of all people. Thus, she would follow through on her word and demonstrate collective good by serving others in the community. More importantly, she helped me understand and embrace my new Western culture. For example, individuality and focusing on oneself seemed … well, selfish. However, Barbara transformed the selfish Western behaviors into actions for greater good.

Simply, Barbara Crocker was a southern belle with style and flair that I had never seen nor experienced in my East Asian culture. Her wardrobe centered around her array of hats, coordinating clothes to her choice of headwear rather than the other way around. In addition to her exquisite wardrobe, Barbara was an extraordinary baker. She was so good that I thought she was *the* Betty Crocker I found in the baking aisle of grocery stores. When I learned she wasn't, I knew why. Her baking was an action of love which could not be packaged. And her baking secrets – like when to sift flour or what she called "add a breath of love," and which parts of the baking pan to grease so that "love can rise freely" – can only be passed down, not bought. I am grateful to have been her apprentice. I've made a commitment to pass down not just her baking secrets but foremost, the life's wisdom she bestowed upon me.

One of them was empowerment. First, Barbara would open my mind by offering a new way to see things. I distinctly remember one time when I asked her what "poor" meant. Calmly, she asked, "Why, honey?" I shared that a boy in my class called me poor when he found out that I had immigrated from South Korea. With a soulful southern smile, she simply explained that "poor" is an adjective. Like "happy" and "sad," adjectives are a temporary state that I can change.

Then, Barbara did something powerful. Not just by words but also with *action*, she showed me how I can change my world. As a speech pathologist for Texas' most marginalized people, she restored people's voices. And the voices she focused on were ones that were not heard – literally and figuratively. I watched her speak – for and on behalf of the voiceless – to the State or any other institutions that were taking advantage of them. She brought me along, training me as she practiced her vocation.

Soon, I was working in many underserved communities suffering from physical illnesses, as well as social illnesses. Together, we served economically poor communities, domestic violence centers for women and their children, restorative organizations for neurodegenerative diseases like Alzheimer's and Parkinson's, and more. As an inquisitive child with unlimited questions of why disparities and injustices exist, she would simply take me to the people who were suffering, and put me to work.

Looking back, I recognized Barbara was a quiet but fierce social justice warrior. She worked tirelessly to fight injustice – particularly racial injustice. As a white woman, she ignored the advice she'd received from banks, institutions, and even her friends who told her to stop working in the "projects." Instead, she took me along and when she wasn't able to serve any longer, I took her place.

I remember one special woman in particular: Ms. Lilly Ruth Warren. Ms. Warren was an elderly African American woman who dedicated her life to a white family as their maid and cook. She never married nor had children. So when she suffered a stroke and there was no family to take care of her, Barbara did. She not only helped to repair Ms. Warren's speech but also thwarted anyone who was exploiting Ms. Warren – the insurance company, the bank and realtors who were after her property, and even the neighborhood kids stealing her food and belongings.

Looking back, I realize I was the recipient of a greater love. I will never forget the Thanksgiving I spent with Ms. Warren. I knew she spent the holidays alone, so I promised I'd be with her. To my surprise when I arrived, Ms. Warren had prepared a picture-perfect Thanksgiving meal, something you'll see on the cover of a gourmet food magazine. Everything was homemade, including the pecan pie. With limited mobility after a stroke, she had cooked for days for her special guest – me! It touched my heart, and she made me feel like a queen as she prepared a meal fit for a queen.

It was then that I began to realize what empowerment is all about. We are empowered when we use our unique skills or abilities to serve and uplift others. It is truly a win–win approach to life as the power it generates when we practice empowerment has a boomerang effect – it comes back to you! For me, I learned that I – an immigrant from a "poor" country, raised by a widow – can have a powerful impact on the lives of others.

Empowerment also requires digging deep and discovering who we truly are. And to see who we truly are, as well as aspire to and become the highest expression of ourselves, we need mirrors – not in the physical sense, but what I call "human truth reflectors." These human mirrors reflect to us our true nature – our character, as well as our fears and doubts. Barbara was my mirror. No matter the problem or self-doubt I brought to her, she would assure me that I was capable of overcoming it. Her mantra was "can," and she in fact told me the word "cannot" didn't exist. It was because of her that I only knew a "can-do" world – one of true empowerment.

Barbara modeled that world with a "can-do" mentality and spirit by showing me how I could build my *muscles of empowerment* through action. From the Parkinson's Foundation to the Projects of Houston, Texas, we took action – serving, uplifting, and empowering the voiceless and the powerless. Together, we worked to empower those whose lives had been impacted by physical disease and, even more, by social consequences of inequity and systemic injustice.

My childhood empowerment training became my way of life and expertise. However, it wasn't until I witnessed the greatest injustice of my life that I became passionate about gender justice and women's empowerment. Barbara was diagnosed with lupus, an autoimmune disease that attacks healthy cells in our own body. Despite Houston having the world's largest medical center, they could not save my Barbara.

So, as an "action-ist" Barbara trained me to be, I took action to find a cure. I went to medical school and graduate school in public health to learn everything I could about the health and wellness of women. But the more I studied, the more I realized that the world had neglected the whole female population. For most medical research, the default setting was male, and the standard prototype in medicine is a twenty-five-year-old 70 kg male. If female physiology was considered, it was reduced to mere body parts, primarily the reproductive organs. Women and minority groups were not included in clinical studies until 1990. Shockingly, even breast cancer research was done on just males before this time. And it came as no surprise that there was a dearth of information on autoimmune diseases, like lupus, given they are more prevalent in women, and black women at that.

My mission to dig deep into women's health and policy led me to the founders of *Our Bodies, Ourselves* (OBOS). *Our Bodies, Ourselves* is a revolutionary publication and movement that awakened women – first, in America and now in twenty-three languages – empowering them to understand and take charge of their own bodies. I lived with one of the founders, listening to their stories and about their revolutionary work. I wanted to learn what worked, and more importantly, what didn't work – why decades after OBOS' first publication, we still do not know so much about women's health and how diseases manifest in the female body.

6.4 Failure Is Success Unrealized

My in-depth research and study on women's health – and the gaps I found in the field – inspired me to propose a comprehensive women's health curriculum for schools of public health (SPH), beginning with where I was studying, the University of California, Berkeley. My master's thesis proposal covered the whole lifespan of females, not just the reproductive years that most of SPH programs covered at the time.

To my surprise, Berkeley rejected this proposal. Their justification was that their existing curriculum – maternal child health (MCH) – was sufficient. Despite all the facts and gaps I laid out, including that MCH was mostly about child health with little on the mother, as well as little to none on adolescent girls, older women, and females without children, they wouldn't budge. They weren't even open to consideration or discussion. Their bottom line was the status quo – that most SPH programs (at the time) were the same.

In order to simply graduate, I prepared an entirely different thesis. This time, it was on adolescent girls' health and development. Coincidentally, another door opened to present my original thesis proposal – although I didn't see it at first.

This is why we need mentors – human mirrors. At this time, I had another amazing mentor. Dr. Patricia Robertson (aka Patty) is a renowned perinatologist (perinatology is an obstetrical subspecialty concerned with the care of the mother and fetus at higher-than-normal risk of complications) and champion of health equity for all. Although she is a phenomenal physician who is invited to make grand rounds across the country, her superpower is the ability to inspire greatness in her students. It's why she was also the Director of Medical Student Education in the Department of Obstetrics, Gynecology & Reproductive Sciences at the University of California San Francisco Medical School.

When Patty learned that UC Berkeley rejected my thesis proposal, she inspired me to present it to a more receptive audience. Specifically, she encouraged me to submit it to a global conference, the International Council on Women's Health Issues. She believed it was the perfect forum to advance women's health.

And yet, I didn't see the wisdom, initially. Preoccupied with finishing my new thesis in order to graduate on time, I missed "seeing the forest for the trees." Furthermore, I was petrified of public speaking – something no one would believe today as I speak around the world.

Like Barbara Crocker, Patty had an extraordinary ability to open the minds of her students. Her special gift is to help young people see beyond the current barriers by focusing on the greater mission. Even when we learned that the conference was on the other side of the globe and with a high registration fee I couldn't afford as a graduate student, she assured me, "We'll find a way!" With the same *can-do* spirit as Barbara, indeed, together, we found a way.

Coincidentally, the conference that year was in Seoul, South Korea, and I was returning to my birthplace. What I didn't know at the time was that it was the beginning of discovering my life's mission. It started with the conference's keynote speaker who was, in fact, the person leading the work my original thesis was based on. Thus, I couldn't help but to approach her and share what I was presenting at the conference – a comprehensive women's health curriculum for the SPH. Then, I offered to be a resource to her work. She replied delightfully, "You speak perfect English!" She must have assumed that I was Korean living in South Korea, not in the United States. I graciously went along, departing with these words, "Yes, I have a lot of skills which I'd like to contribute to advance the mission of your work." And that is exactly what happened.

6.5 Crisis = Danger + Opportunity

The September 11 attacks shocked the world and rocked the United States of America. The horrific attack on our homeland and everything America stands for united the nation and galvanized the world. National security became our #1 priority, inspiring something that's rarely done in Washington, DC – action! Focusing on the safety and security of Americans, particularly the most vulnerable groups, I made a compelling case for one such group – girls.

This was possible because the keynote speaker I met at the International Council on Women's Health Issues conference was the Assistant Secretary of Health on Women's Health. Established in 1991, Dr. Wanda Jones led one of the first federal offices dedicated to women and girls. And given the Office's focus has been mostly on adult women, they were in fact seeking expertise on other age groups, most importantly adolescent girls and young women.

So, I moved to Washington, DC, to work in the Office on Women's Health, the Office of Secretary, the US Department of Health and Human Services – serving our nation's girls. Working directly with world renowned institutions like the National Institutes of Health and the Centers for Disease Control and Prevention, as well as having access to the rest of the executive branch, including the White House, I felt like a kid in a candy store, wanting to taste it all regardless of how sick I'd get.

Indeed, it made me sick. Politics made me sick. Washington was all about power, and girls held no power. Words were just rhetoric, and when people learned that my work focused on girls, they'd condescendingly comment, "That's so nice."

During those years, I would remember what Barbara taught me: "You don't have to win all the battles. Just win the war." And to win wars, you need a strategy. (In fact, the word "strategy" came from military operations in a war.) First, make your cause known. To do this in Washington, DC, I showed up at other people's meetings and agendas, supporting and aligning with them, as well as seeking potential collaboration or partnership. This led them to include my cause on the agenda.

Second, change the storyline about your cause, particularly if no one is paying attention to the existing storyline. That is, girls were depicted as weak and powerless, particularly in economically poor countries. We can all remember television ads of poverty-stricken girls with runny noses. Coincidently at the time, a group of experts was gathering to change this storyline. With a particular focus on adolescent girls in the developing world, the goal was to change the narrative – from one of powerlessness to a powerful force for change and sustainability.

Then, as if on cue, international and multilateral organizations began to release data showing that girls' empowerment, mainly via education, has the best return on investment when it comes to global development.[4] For example, each year a girl is educated, her earning potential increases by 10 to 20 percent. Secondary education is even more powerful, doubling her income potential.[5] In fact, if every girl on the planet received 12 years of quality education, their earning potential would add $15 to $30 trillion – with a "T" – to the global economy.[3]

Yes, empowered girls are a powerful solution to the crises of our planet and a better world. Furthermore, girls' empowerment goes beyond the global SDGs. Leadership training and experiences rooted in service and social justice action – as I've been taught and still practice today – build the *muscles of empowerment*.

A model program is Girl Scouts. Serving 2.3 million girls in the United States, with sister organizations serving 10 million girls around the world, the Girl Scouts USA is a premier girls' leadership development program boasting an extraordinary alumnae base – including Michelle Obama, Hillary Clinton, Condoleezza Rice, Supreme Court Justice Sandra Day O'Connor, American astronaut Sally Ride, Taylor Swift, Serena and Venus Williams, 76 percent of female senators, and 80 percent of female governors.[7] Thus, I was thrilled and honored when they recruited me to head and lead their new Global Action program. The year I joined their team, 83 percent of women in the US Congress were former Girl Scouts!

6.6 A Disposal Population or a Game Changer?

Although empowered girls are a powerful force for change, until our world recognizes it, girls – especially the most marginalized and disadvantaged – will continue to live in a brutal, discriminating world. This reality was clearly stated to me by a global development expert whom I met at a conference. When he asked me about my work, I answered, "I develop future empowered female leaders," adding a passionate elevator speech that this is the most powerful solution to poverty, climate crisis, conflict, and even national security. As we went our separate ways, he gave me his email address with these parting words, "I commend you for your work. The population you are advocating for is the 'disposable' population."

Girls are disposable. Hearing these words was shocking. And yet, it's true. Our world sees and treats girls as disposable – exploit, sell, rape, and kill them with impunity. It is in fact how we've created such a gender-imbalanced world.

With this said, how dare he call girls *disposable*? With passion and anger to prove him wrong, I wrote a 2AM email, highlighting key data, particularly on poverty and economic growth as this was his mission. I showed girls' empowerment is vital to his work and sustainability. I signed off by extending an invitation to work together – for girls in his country.

A few weeks later I received a reply from his organization. It stated that I had met their chairman who founded their organization, which has impacted the lives of 100 million people in poor countries, globally, including their home country of Bangladesh. Then, they invited me to come to Bangladesh to train them – serving nearly a quarter of million girls – in girls' leadership development.

So, who did I meet?

Sir Fazle Hasan Abed, KCMG (the honorary British Order awarded for extraordinary service in a foreign country) is the founder of BRAC, the world's largest nongovernmental organization with over 120,000 employees. Learning that BRAC was founded the year I was born, I wholeheartedly understood what he meant by "girls are disposable." I too would have been "disposed" as a baby girl without a father.

At the same time, I was also surprised that BRAC, a well known sustainable development model, was not aware of girls' leadership development and its powerful impact on societies. Indeed, girls' empowerment is a game changer. Empowered girls will become future leaders who will transform Bangladesh. So I went to Bangladesh to take action with them!

6.7 The Real Power of Empowerment

The power of girls' empowerment is indisputable. I started 4GGL to ignite the next generation of *empowered* women changemakers, glocally – global mission, local action (see Figure 26). In less than one year, I received training and partnership requests from grassroots organizations serving over 500,000 girls around the globe. Just like BRAC, they were all inspired by 4GGL's vision, mission, and approach and were seeking training in what was novel and innovative to them – girls' leadership development.

Feeling responsible for the possibility that I could help change the trajectory of half a million girls' lives, I worked nonstop. Being born in the East and raised in the West, I felt doubly responsible. My East Asian ethos infused duty and obligation into my DNA. This was combined with my Western upbringing, which acculturated agency and self-determination of all human beings. Thus, I poured all my energy and resources into action, exceeding the 10,000 hours that have been equated with expertise. Indeed, I could prove it, as I can do the training in my sleep. I'd get off the plane in the country of the partner organization, ready to train and take action with them.

Figure 26 A drawing of Jin In and 4GGL.

Source: Drawn for the Element by Gabriela Cordero Durán, used with permission.

However, all this action came at a deleterious cost. I sacrificed my own basic needs like sleep, rest and relaxation, and even health care – for a greater mission. Indeed, I became a martyr to the cause, and it led to a great challenge and a new reality with which I had to live. I was diagnosed with hypothyroidism – literally, the depletion of energy.

Life challenges are our most powerful teachers. They are our wake-up calls and learning opportunities for powerful transformation. As I was literally running out of physical energy, my mental and spiritual energy was heightened, giving me a deeper understanding about power.

The problem is power; the solution is to empower.

First, the problem is power; the solution is to empower. Whether gender inequality or any other inequality or injustice, at the core of the problem is an imbalance and hoarding of power – of one group *over* another. This has resulted in systemic and systematic inequities that are pervasive and incessant in societies. The way forward is to empower or, more precisely, to restore the inherent power, worth, and dignity of those whose power has been taken away.

Second, to truly know and understand power, we must also know and understand *powerlessness*. It is in knowing powerlessness that we use power appropriately – power for a greater good and power *with* others, rather than power just for ourselves or power *over* others.

Third and lastly, at the core of all social diseases is a virus – a fundamental mindset that is antiquated and patriarchal. For example, whether teen pregnancy in some countries or child marriage in others, the disease or the root cause is the same – a toxic mindset that devalues, degrades, and dehumanizes girls.

Therefore, the treatment requires a new level of consciousness. And the most powerful and dominant sensory organ is vision. That is, what we see, or as behavioral economist and a recipient of the Nobel Memorial Prize in Economic Sciences, Daniel Kahneman, says, "What we see is all there is."

This Element is to *show* the world the most powerful force for change: *Girl Power*. With pioneering data – the first-ever globally collected on women's empowerment – as well as powerful case studies of Girl Power in action, my hope is to make empowerment concrete. That is, rather than some rhetoric or wishful thinking, we can turn empowerment into concrete muscles that every girl and young woman – or anyone, for that matter – can build. Only then is empowerment truly attainable and realizable.

Finally, unlike power, true empowerment is for the collective, and cannot be hoarded by a single individual or one group. This is how we can bring about systemic change. It's why 4GGL has gone beyond a charitable organization. It is a social change movement – revolutionizing the toxic mindset that devalues and dehumanizes girls into a new paradigm that realizes empowered girls are a powerful force for change. Like all social injustices and inequities, societal transformation requires a movement where every person takes accountability and action – now!

References

1. Chaucer, G. *The Canterbury tales*. (Penguin Books, 2007).
2. King, Martin Luther. *Where do we go from here: Chaos or community?* (Harper & Row, 1967).
3. Page, N. & Czuba, C. Empowerment: What is it? *J. Ext.* **37**, 1–5 (1999).
4. Richardson, D. *Conceptualising gender: Introducing gender and women's studies*. (Macmillan International, 2020).
5. Jayakarani, R., Hennink, M., Kiiti, N., Pillinger, M. & Jayakaran, R. Defining empowerment: Perspectives from international development organisations. *Dev. Pract.* **22**, 202–215 (2012).
6. World Bank. *Population-total – world*. https://data.worldbank.org/indica tor/SP.POP.TOTL?locations=1W (2023).
7. Carvalho, A. B., Sampaio, M. C., Varandas, F. R. & Klaczko, L. B. An experimental demonstration of Fisher's principle: Evolution of sexual proportion by natural selection. *Genetics* **148**, 719–731 (1998).
8. UNFPA. *Lives together, worlds apart: Men and women in a time of change*. www.unfpa.org/publications/state-world-population-2000 (2000).
9. Chesler, P. *Worldwide trends in honor killings*. www.meforum.org/2646/ worldwide-trends-in-honor-killings (2010).
10. Iyengar, R. Indian minister says 2,000 girls are killed across the country every day. *Time*, 48 (2015).
11. James Madison University. *Gendercide: An issue all of us should be aware of*. Shout out. https://bit.ly/43MzOP5 (2014).
12. Hesketh, T. & Xing, Z. W. Abnormal sex ratios in human populations: Causes and consequences. *Proc. Natl. Acad. Sci.* **103**, 13271–13275 (2006).
13. World Bank. *Population – Male*. https://bit.ly/43I1EMj (2023).
14. Leaders. Gendercide. *The Economist* (2010, March 6).
15. UNFPA. *Gender-biased sex selection*. www.unfpa.org/gender-biased-sex-selection#readmore-expand (2020).
16. Bongaarts, J. & Guilmoto, C. Z. How many more missing women? Excess female mortality and prenatal sex selection, 1970–2050. *Popul. Dev. Rev.* **41**, 241–269 (2015).
17. Basu, M. & Merrill, C. *A girl gets married every 2 seconds somewhere in the world*. CNN Health. www.cnn.com/2018/01/29/health/child-marriage-by-the-numbers/index.html (2018).
18. UNFPA West and Central Africa Regional Office. *7 things you might not know about child marriage*. News. https://bit.ly/43MLtxc (2020).

19. Department of Justice. *Office of Justice programs, Bureau of Justice statistics, sex offenses and offenders.* (Department of Justice, 1997).

20. United Nations Office on Drugs and Crime. *2020 saw a woman or girl being killed by someone in their family every 11 minutes.* https://bit.ly/4aDgXYO (2021).

21. Girls Not Brides. www.girlsnotbrides.org/ (2023).

22. Béné, C. & Merten, S. Women and fish-for-sex: Transactional sex, HIV/AIDS and gender in African fisheries. *World Dev.* **36**, 875–899 (2008).

23. Abrahams, N., Mhlongo, S., Chirwa, E., et al. Femicide, intimate partner femicide, and non-intimate partner femicide in South Africa: An analysis of 3 national surveys, 1999–2017. *Plos One Med.* **21** (2024).

24. Reis, C. & Meyer, S. R. Understudied and underaddressed: Femicide, an extreme form of violence against women and girls. *Plos One Med.* **21** (2024).

25. Goldin, C. *Gender gap.* The Library of Economics and Liberty. www.econlib.org/library/Enc/GenderGap.html (2019).

26. WEF. *Global Gender Gap Report 2023.* www3.weforum.org/docs/WEF_GGGR_2023.pdf (2023).

27. UN Women and UNDP. *Expert's take: Most of the world's women and girls struggle with large gaps in equality and empowerment.* https://bit.ly/3TIfwBG (2019).

28. Arsht-Rock. *The scorching divide: How extreme heat inflames gender inequalities in health and income.* One Billion Resilient. https://onebillionresilient.org/extreme-heat-inflames-gender-inequalities/ (2023).

29. ILO. *Rural women at work: Bridging the gap.* https://bit.ly/43P4pv9 (2017).

30. FAO. *The role of women in agriculture.* www.fao.org/3/am307e/am307e00.pdf (2011).

31. UNDP. *What does gender equality have to do with climate change?* News and Stories. https://bit.ly/43MzUGr (2023).

32. FAO. *The state of food and agriculture 2010–2011: Women in agriculture: Closing the gender gap for development.* www.fao.org/docrep/013/i2050e/i2050e00.htm (2011).

33. Gates, M. F. Putting women and girls at the center of development. *Science (80–)* **345**, 1273–1275 (2014).

34. Mavisakalyan, A. & Tarverdi, Y. Gender and climate change: Do female parliamentarians make difference? *Eur. J. Polit. Econ.* **56**, 151–164 (2019).

35. Haas, T. *Women reclaiming the city international research on urbanism, architecture, and planning.* (Rowman & Littlefield, 2023).

36. The Project Drawdown. *Family, planning and education.* Health and Education. www.drawdown.org/solutions/family-planning-and-education (2023).

37. Kwauk, C. & Braga, A. *Three platforms for girls' education in climate strategies*. Brookings. https://bit.ly/4cAPhpc (2017).

38. Redmore, L. E. *(Re)claiming forestry: A case study of women's empowerment* (Master's thesis, Oregon State University, 2009).

39. Begum, F., Bruyn, L. L. de, Kristiansen, P. & Islam, M. A. Forest co-management in the Sundarban mangrove forest: Impacts of women's participation on their livelihoods and sustainable forest resource conservation. *Environ. Dev.* **43**, 100731 (2022).

40. Carr, M. & Hartl, M. *Gender and non-timber forest products: Promoting food security and economic empowerment*. Food and Agriculture Organization of the United Nations. https://bit.ly/3VFftZT (2008).

41. Davis, R. & Silver, M. *How women in a fishing village are fighting for power*. NPR. https://bit.ly/3vupYoh (2019).

42. Salim, S. S. & Rajamanickam, G. Empowerment of fisherwomen in Kerala: An assessment. *Indian J. Fish.* **60**, 73–80 (2013).

43. Nathenson, P., Slater, S., Higdon, P., Aldinger, C. & Ostheimer, E. No sex for fish: Empowering women to promote health and economic opportunity in a localized place in Kenya. *Health Promot. Int.* **32**, 800–807 (2017).

44. Kumar, P. & Igdalsky, L. Sustained uptake of clean cooking practices in poor communities: Role of social networks. *Energy Res. Soc. Sci.* **48**, 189–193 (2019).

45. Asian Development Bank. *Energy for all: Addressing the energy, environment, and poverty nexus in Asia*. https://bit.ly/3xmJtj7 (2007).

46. Juntarawijit, Y. & Juntarawijit, C. Cooking smoke exposure and respiratory symptoms among those responsible for household cooking: A study in Phitsanulok, Thailand. *Heliyon* **5**, e01706 (2019).

47. Polsky, D. & Ly, C. *Consequences of indoor air pollution: A review of the solutions and challenges*. (Alliance for Clean Cookstoves, 2012).

48. Lim, Stephen S., Vos, T., Flaxman, A., et al. A comparative risk assessment of burden of disease and injury attributable to 67 risk factors and risk factor clusters in 21 regions, 1990–2010: A systematic analysis for the Global Burden of Disease Study 2010. *Lancet* **380**, 2224–2260 (2012).

49. Smith, K. R., Bruce, N., Balakrishnan, K., et al. Millions dead: how do we know and what does it mean? Methods used in the comparative risk assessment of household air pollution. *Annu. Rev. Public Heal.* **35**, 185–206 (2014).

50. Sovacool, B. K. & Griffiths, S. The cultural barriers to a low-carbon future: A review of six mobility and energy transitions across 28 countries. *Renew. Sustain. Energy Rev.* **119** (2020).

51. Gaye, A. *Access to energy and human development 2007/2008*. https://purocihle.rrojasdatabank.info/gaye_amie.pdf (2007).

52. Reddy, B. S., Balachandra, P. & Nathan, H. S. K. Universalization of access to modern energy services in Indian households: Economic and policy analysis. *Energy Policy* **37**, 4645–4657 (2009).

53. Sagar, A. D. Alleviating energy poverty for the world's poor. *Energy Policy* **33**, 1367–1372 (2005).

54. Laxmi, V., Parikh, J., Karmakar, S. & Dabrase, P. Household energy, women's hardship and health impacts in rural Rajasthan, India: Need for sustainable energy solutions. *Energy Sustain. Dev.* **7**, 50–68 (2003).

55. Sovacool, B. K. *Energy, poverty, and development*. (Routledge, 2014).

56. Barnes, D. F. *The challenge of rural electrification: Strategies for developing countries*. (Routledge, 2007).

57. Barnes, D. F. & Sen, M. *The impact of energy on women's lives in rural India*. (Washington, DC: World Bank, 2004).

58. Misana, S. & Karlsson, G. V. *Generating opportunities: Case studies on energy and women*. (United Nations Development Programme, 2001).

59. United Nations Development Program. *Gender and energy toolkit*. (2004).

60. Sovacool, B. K. & Drupady, I. M. Summoning earth and fire: The energy development implications of Grameen Shakti (GS) in Bangladesh. *Energy* **36**, 4445–4459 (2011).

61. Mekonnen, M. & Hoekstra, A. Four billion people facing severe water scarcity. *Sci. Adv.* **2** (2016).

62. Water.org. *How does the world water crisis affect women and girls?* A women's crisis. https://water.org/our-impact/water-crisis/womens-crisis/ (2016).

63. Sinharoy, S. S. & Caruso, B. A. On World Water Day, gender equality and empowerment require attention. *Lancet Planet. Heal.* **3** (2019).

64. Graham, J. P., Hirai, M. & Kim, S.-S. An analysis of water collection labor among women and children in 24 sub-Saharan African countries. *PLoS One* **11**, e0155981 (2016).

65. Sorenson, S. B., Morssink, C. & Campos, P. A. Safe access to safe water in low income countries: Water fetching in current times. *Soc. Sci. Med.* **72**, 1522–1526 (2011).

66. Bisung, E. & Elliott, S. J. Psychosocial impacts of the lack of access to water and sanitation in low- and middle-income countries: A scoping review. *J. Water Health* **15** (2017).

67. Deepa, J. & Fawcet, B. Water projects and women's empowerment. In Scott, R. (ed.), *People and systems for water, sanitation and health: Proceedings of the 27th WEDC International Conference*, Lusaka, Zambia, 20–24 August, pp. 423–426 (2001). https://hdl.handle.net/2134/29197.

68. Aladuwaka, S. & Momsen, J. Sustainable development, water resources management and women's empowerment: The Wanaraniya Water Project in Sri Lanka. *Gend. Dev.* **18**, 43–58 (2010).

69. Leder, S., Clement, F. & Karki, E. Reframing women's empowerment in water security programmes in Western Nepal. *Gend. Dev.* **25**, 235–251 (2017).

70. Naiga, R., Ananga, E. O. & Kakumba, U. Gendered participation in water governance: Implications for successful community-based water management and women empowerment. *Int. J. Rural Manag.* **0** (2023).

71. UNICEF. Twenty-five years of progress for women since the Beijing Declaration. https://bit.ly/3UwMypK (2020).

72. Napp, C. & Breda, T. The stereotype that girls lack talent: A worldwide investigation. *Sci. Adv.* **8** (2022).

73. Lawson, M. A., Martin, A. E., Huda, I. & Matz, S. C. Hiring women into senior leadership positions is associated with a reduction in gender stereotypes in organizational language. *Proc. Natl. Acad. Sci.* **119**, e2026443119 (2022).

74. Graves Jr, J. L. G., Kearney, M., Barabino, G. & Malcom, S. Inequality in science and the case for a new agenda. *Proc. Natl. Acad. Sci.* **119**, e2117831119 (2022).

75. Vlasceanu, M. & Amodio, D. M. Propagation of societal gender inequality by internet search algorithms. *Proc. Natl. Acad. Sci.* **119**, e2204529119 (2022).

76. Sarant, L. The gender divide: Agents of change. *Nature* **549**, S70–S74 (2017).

77. Donneys, C. O. & Perea, J. D. Empowering Afro-Indigenous girls. *Science (80–.)* **375**, 730 (2022).

78. UNICEF. *Girls' education*. Programme. www.unicef.org/education/girls-education (2023).

79. World Bank. *Missed opportunities: The high cost of not educating girls*. https://bit.ly/49RI0Pd (2018).

80. Bank, T. W. *Unrealized potential: The high cost of gender inequality in earnings*. https://bit.ly/49S9T9K (2018).

81. McKinsey Global Institute. *How advancing women's equality can add $12 trillion to global growth*. https://bit.ly/4aQXQLg (2015).

82. World Economic Forum. *The global gender gap report*. www.weforum.org/publications/global-gender-gap-report-2023/ (2023).

83. World Bank. *World development report 2012: Gender equality and development*. http://elibrary.worldbank.org/doi/book/10.1596/978-0-8213-8810-5 (2012).

84. World Bank. *Women, business and the law.* https://wbl.worldbank.org/en/wbl (2016).

85. UN Women. *Facts and figures: HIV and AIDS.* www.unwomen.org/en/what-we-do/hiv-and-aids/facts-and-figures#notes (2016).

86. UNICEF. *Female genital mutilation (FGM).* https://data.unicef.org/topic/child-protection/female-genital-mutilation/ (2023).

87. Cappa, C., Moneti, F., Wardlaw, T. & Bissell, S. Elimination of female genital mutilation/cutting. *Lancet* **382**, 1080–1081 (2013).

88. Klein, E., Helzner, E., Shayowitz, M., Kohlhoff, S. & Smith-Norowitz, T. A. Genital mutilation: Health consequences and complications: A short literature review. *Obstet. Gynecol. Int.* 7365715 (2018). https://doi.org/10.1155/2018/7365715.

89. WHO/UNICEF/UNFPA. *Female genital mutilation: A joint WHO/UNICEF/UNFPA statement.* https://iris.who.int/handle/10665/41903 (1997).

90. Berg, R. C. & Underland, V. The obstetric consequences of female genital mutilation/cutting: A systematic review and meta-analysis. *Obstet. Gynecol. Int.*, 1–15 (2013). https://doi.org/10.1155/2013/496564.

91. Mulongo, P., Martin, C. H. & McAndrew, S. The psychological impact of female genital mutilation/cutting (FGM/C) on girls/women's mental health: A narrative literature review. *J. Reprod. Infant Psychol.* **32**, 469–485 (2014).

92. WHO study group on female genital mutilation and obstetric outcome et al. Female genital mutilation and obstetric outcome: WHO collaborative prospective study in six African countries. *Lancet* **367**, 1835–1841 (2006).

93. Smith, L. C., Khan, F., Frankenberger, T. R., et al. Admissible evidence in the court of development evaluation? The impact of care's Shouhardo Project on child stunting in Bangladesh. *World Dev.* **41**, 196–216 (2011).

94. Langer, A., Meleis, A., Knaul, F. M., et al. Women and health: the key for sustainable development. *Lancet* **386**, 1165–1210 (2015).

95. UNOCD. *Global report on trafficking in persons.* https://bit.ly/3w99nqg (2018).

96. ILO. *Profits and poverty: The economics of forced labour.* https://bit.ly/3WfrPs6 (2014).

97. Walk Free. *Stacked odds.* https://bit.ly/4b86lkN (2020).

98. Ricaforte, M. *Why women are more likely to be impacted by human trafficking.* Dressember. www.dressember.org/blog/dressemberreading 3 (2020).

99. Bhattacharya, A. *ISIL's human traffickers are using Facebook, WhatsApp, and Telegram to sell slaves.* Quartz. https://qz.com/777152/isil-is-using-facebook-fb-whatsapp-and-telegram-to-sell-slaves (2016).

100. Global Peace Index 2023. *Institute for Economics & Peace.* www.vision ofhumanity.org/wp-content/uploads/2023/06/GPI-2023-Web.pdf (2023).

101. Hudson, V. M., Caprioli, M., Ballif-Spanvill, B., McDermott, R. & Emmett, C. F. The heart of the matter: The security of women and the security of states. *Int. Secur.* **33**, 7–45 (2008).

102. Hudson, V. M. *What sex means for world peace.* Foreign Policy. https://foreignpolicy.com/2012/04/24/what-sex-means-for-world-peace/ (2012).

103. Washington State for Public Policy. *Washington's offender accountability act: Department of Corrections' static risk instrument.* https://bit.ly/3wa7MRa (2007).

104. Cliff, A. *A future world.* DAZED. https://bit.ly/44CJoUN (2019).

105. Martiskainen, M., Axon, S., Sovacool, B. K., et al. Contextualizing climate justice activism: knowledge, emotions, motivations, and actions among climate strikers in six cities. *Glob. Environ. Chang.* (2020) https://doi.org/10.1016/j.gloenvcha.2020.102180.

106. Thunberg, G. Speech to the European Commission. (2019).

107. The Hong Kong Special Administrative Region. *Basic law.* www.basic law.gov.hk/en/basiclaw/index.html (2023).

108. BBC. *The Hong Kong protests explained in 100 and 500 words.* China. www.bbc.co.uk/news/world-asia-china-49317695 (2019).

109. Chan, H. Explainer: Hong Kong's five demands: Universal suffrage. *Hong Kong Free Press* https://hongkongfp.com/2019/12/26/explainer-hong-kongs-five-demands-universal-suffrage/ (2020).

110. Reuters. US and UK condemn arrest of Hong Kong democracy activists. *The Guardian* (2020).

111. BBC. *Hong Kong national security law: What is it and is it worrying?* News. www.bbc.co.uk/news/world-asia-china-52765838 (2022).

112. NHK World – Japan. *"Be water": Hong Kong protesters learn from Bruce Lee.* News2. www3.nhk.or.jp/nhkworld/en/news/backstories/745/ (2019).

113. Engelbrecht, C., Marcolini, B., Tiefenthäler, A., Al-Hlou, Y. & Chow, Y. Meet the students fueling Hong Kong's protests: "We may die." *New York Times* (2019).

114. Hao, A. Young women are front and center in the Hong Kong protests. *Teen Vogue* (2019).

115. Tsoi, G. *"Shield Girl": The face of Hong Kong's anti-extradition movement.* BBC. www.bbc.co.uk/news/world-asia-china-48604933 (2019).

116. Lau, J. Hong Kong is still waiting for its feminist uprising. *The Nation* (2020).

117. Ng, J. Chinese propaganda paints Hong Kong as a spoiled brat. *Foreign Policy* (2019).

118. Anderson, L. *Afghanistan is most dangerous country for women*. Reuters. www.reuters.com/article/us-women-danger-idUSTRE75E31R20110615 (2011).

119. Gresko, J. Afghan girls robotics team competes after visa obstacles. *USA Today* (2017).

120. George, S. Afghan forces are claiming victory in some Taliban-controlled areas. Civilians say they're still in danger. *Washington Post* (2020).

121. UNFPA. Afghanistan: *Young people: What we do*. https://afghanistan .unfpa.org/en/node/15227 (2022).

122. Mahboob, R. Empower and educate Afghanistan's youth to ensure a peaceful future. *New York Times* (2019).

123. Oslo Freedom Forum. *Fatemah Qaderyan | The Afghan Dreamers*. (YouTube, 2018).

124. Stahl, L. *The Chibok girls: Survivors of kidnapping by Boko Haram share their stories*. CBS News. https://bit.ly/3xJpPOj (2019).

125. Amnesty International. *Nigeria: Starving women raped by soldiers and militia who claim to be rescuing them*. News. https://bit.ly/4d9y3zB (2018).

126. Maclean, R. & Abrak, I. Boko Haram returns more than 100 schoolgirls kidnapped last month. *The Guardian* (2018).

127. Amnesty International. *Nigeria: Abducted women and girls forced to join Boko Haram attacks*. News. https://bit.ly/49Sefh6 (2015).

128. Amnesty International. *Nigeria: Eight years after Chibok more than 1,500 children abducted by armed groups*. Press Release. https://bit.ly/ 3U8E4DY (2014).

129. UNICEF. *More than 1,000 children in northeastern Nigeria abducted by Boko Haram since 2013*. Press Release. https://bit.ly/4aLUdGs (2018).

130. Hudson, V. M., Ballif-Spanvill, B., Caprioli, M. & Emmett, C. F. *Sex and world peace*. (Columbia University Press, 2014). https://doi.org/10.7312/ huds13182.

131. UN Women. *Preventing violent extremism and countering terrorism*. Peace and Security. https://bit.ly/4aNXDbD (2023).

132. Vogelstein, R. B. & Bigio, J. *Women and terrorism: Hidden threats, forgotten partners*. Council on Foreign Relations. www.cfr.org/blog/ women-and-terrorism-hidden-threats-forgotten-partners (2019).

133. Hayes, C. "We're not backing down": One month after shooting, Parkland student movement picking up steam. *USA Today* (2018).

134. March for Our Lives. *Our Mission* https://marchforourlives.com/mission-story/ (2023).

135. North, A. *"Teenagers don't really take no for an answer": Young activists see a turning point on guns.* The Vox. https://bit.ly/3w4GITl (2018).

136. Johnson, A. *Florida school shooting: Teachers describe chaos as students fled gunman.* NBC News. https://bit.ly/3w7cIWO (2018).

137. Martin, M. *2019 has seen more mass shootings than days on the calendar.* NPR. https://bit.ly/3y21OSE (2019).

138. Aradillas, E. What to know about Jaclyn Corin, class president who became national activist after school shooting. *People* (2018).

139. Bromwich, J. E. How the Parkland students got so good at social media. *New York Times* (2018).

140. Leitner, T. & Silva, D. *Parkland students travel to Florida capital to push gun law reform.* NBC News. https://bit.ly/3yjRNAr (2018).

141. Adeyina, S. I helped organize the "March for Our Lives" because there is strength in numbers. *Seventeen* (2018).

142. Gifford Law Center to Prevent Gun Violence. *Statistics.* https://giffords.org/lawcenter/gun-violence-statistics/ (2023).

143. Politi, D. *March for Our Lives put Sarah Chadwick's spoof NRA ad on the big screen and it was glorious.* Slate. https://bit.ly/3U6zxlu (2018).

144. Kaleem, J. & Agrawal, N. These are the Florida students behind the movement to end gun violence. *Los Angeles Times* (2018).

145. Perez, M. *Parkland student slams NRA for promoting gun that looks like cellphone on website.* NewsWeek. www.newsweek.com/parkland-guns-nra-cell-phone-907674 (2018).

146. Fox, K. *How US gun culture compares with the world.* CNN. https://edition.cnn.com/2017/10/03/americas/us-gun-statistics/index.html (2019).

147. Karp, A. *Estimating global civilian-held firearms numbers.* Small Arms Survey. https://bit.ly/49RippI (2018).

148. Grinshteyn, E. & Hemenway, D. Violent death rates: The US compared with other high-income OECD countries, 2010. *Am. J. Med.* **129**, 266–273 (2015).

149. Fox, J. A. & Fridel, E. E. The tenuous connections involving mass shootings, mental illness, and gun laws. *Violence Gend.* **30** (2016).

150. Gold, L. H. Domestic violence, firearms, and mass shootings. *J. Am. Acad. Psychiatry Law Online* **48** (2020).

151. FBI. *Crime in the U.S. 2016.* Crime in the US. https://bit.ly/4aUvShN (2016).

152. Washington State Institute for Public Policy. *No Washington's offender accountability act.* https://bit.ly/4bsA1JL (2008).

153. Statista Research Department. *Number of mass shootings in the United States between 1982 and August 2023, by shooter's gender.* Crime & Law Enforcement. https://bit.ly/49Qzv7e (2023).

154. Goldberg, E. *Nada Al-Ahdal, Yemeni girl who evaded child marriage, says she'd "rather die" than get married off (VIDEO).* Huffington Post. www.huffpost.com/entry/nada-al-ahdal-child-bride_n_3634468 (2013).

155. Nada al-Ahdal. *Remember Nada Al-Ahdal? Here she is today.* https://bit .ly/49NIwh7 (2019).

156. Memri TV Videos. *11-year-old Yemeni girl Nada Al-Ahdal flees home to avoid forced marriage: I'd rather kill myself.* YouTube. (2016).

157. Letsoalo, I. *6 activists who are fighting child marriage in their countries.* Demand Equity. www.globalcitizen.org/en/content/child-marriage-women-activists-africa/ (2019).

158. Alahdal, N. *Yemeni girl's fight against forced marriage going viral.* YouTube. (2016).

159. Nada Foundation. *The rights of women in the Middle East.* https://nada fund.org/home (2020).

160. Saleh, S. A. "Early marriage fears of Nada Al-Ahdal are fabricated" says her parents, interior ministry officials, and prominent child rights NGO. *Yemen Post* (2013).

161. Alahdal, N. *She was kidnapped by al-Qaeda, placed under house arrest and arrested by Interior Ministry.* YouTube. (2017).

162. The Borgen Project. *5 activists ending child marriages.* Latest news. https://borgenproject.org/5-activists-ending-child-marriages/ (2019).

163. Nada Foundation. *The life march of the girl Nada Al-hdal.* https://nada fund.org/2019/02/08/the-life-march-of-the-girl-nada-al-hdal.html (2019).

164. Equality Now. *Child marriage in the United States.* www.equalitynow .org/learn_more_child_marriage_us/ (2020).

165. UNICEF. *Yemen country brief.* www.unicef.org/mena/media/1821/file/ MENA-CMReport-YemenBrief.pdf.pdf (2017).

166. UNICEF. *Is an end to child marriage within reach?* https://data.unicef .org/resources/is-an-end-to-child-marriage-within-reach/ (2023).

167. ActionAid. *Women and stigma.* https://drive.google.com/file/d/ 1bdivjRlweAif8_AJBsA9QjgCjpEp3t3s/view?pli=1 (2022).

168. DivChata. *The history of NGO girls.* www.divchata.org/en/about-us/the-history-of-divchata.html (2023).

169. Foroudi, L. *Rising domestic violence is a hidden front in Ukraine's war.* Reuters. https://bit.ly/4d9zVZ9 (2023).

170. Cornwall, A. Women's empowerment: What works? *J. Int. Dev.,* **28**, 342–359 (2016).

171. US Department of State. *Office of Global Women's Issues*. Washington, DC. https://bit.ly/3UzxJmA (2023).

172. Alsop, R., Heinsohn, N., & Somma, A. Measuring empowerment: An analytic framework. In Alsop, R. (ed.), *Power, Rights and Poverty: Concepts and Connections*. (World Bank, 2005).

173. United Nations. *Gender Parity Strategy*. Geneva, October 2017. https://bit.ly/4aSC9dK.

174. Reshi, I. A. & Sudha, T. Women empowerment: A literature review. *IJEBAS* **2**(6), 1353–1359 (2022). https://doi.org/10.54443/ijebas.v2i6.753.

175. Reshi, I. A., Sudha, T., & Dar, S. A. Women's access to education and its impact on their empowerment: A comprehensive review. *MORFAI Journal* **1**(2), 446–450 (2022). https://doi.org/10.54443/morfai.v1i2.760.

176. Sundaram, M. S., Sekar, M., & Subburaj, A. Women empowerment: Role of education. *IJMSS* **2**(12), 76–85 (2014).

177. Perper, R. *Hong Kong protesters say they are prepared to fight for democracy "until we win, or we die."* Business Insider. https://bit.ly/49Ucyjv (2019).

178. Truesdell, J., & Truesdell, J. Parkland school shooting survivors David and Lauren Hogg write in book: "When it happened to us, we woke up." *People*. https://bit.ly/49Wuj1z (2018).

179. Whitney, S. A Parkland shooting survivor to adults: "We need you." *Glamour*. www.glamour.com/story/parkland-survivor-message-to-adults (2018).

180. United Nations. *The four pillars of United Nations Security Council Resolution 1325*. UNOAU. https://bit.ly/3Qkev1L (2021).

181. O'Reilly, M., Ó, S. A., & Paffenholz, T. *Reimagining peacemaking: Women's roles in Peace processes*. https://bit.ly/3WdtWwe (2015).

182. World Bank. *Gender equality: Achieve gender equality and empower all women and girl*. https://bit.ly/3WfgVCp (2017).

183. World Bank. *Women, business and the law*. https://wbl.worldbank.org/en/wbl (2018).

184. Chenoweth, E. & Stepha, M. J. *Why civil resistance works: The strategic logic of nonviolent conflict*. (Columbia University Press, 2012).

185. Hugo, V. *The future of man: From the series Great Ideas of Western Man*. (Washington, DC: Smithsonian Institute, 1964).

186. UNDP. *The paths to equal: New twin indices on gender equality and women's empowerment*. https://bit.ly/3UtpY1j (2015).

187. Plan International. *Girls and COVID-19*. https://plan-international.org/publications/living-under-lockdown (2020).

188. UN Women. The Shadow Pandemic: Violence against women during COVID-19. https://bit.ly/4db4m18 (2020).

189. Wittenberg-Cox, A. *What do countries with the best coronavirus responses have in common?* Forbes. https://bit.ly/4b6ZEQ7 (2020).

190. Taub, A. Why are women-led nations doing better with Covid-19? *New York Times.* www.nytimes.com/2020/05/15/world/coronavirus-women-leaders.html (2020).

191. Musgrave, P. *Afghan teenage girls innovate low cost ventilator.* The Borgen Project. https://borgenproject.org/tag/the-afghan-dreamers/ (2020).

192. Ebrahimji, A. *Greta Thunberg is donating $100,000 to help children affected by coronavirus pandemic.* CNN News. https://bit.ly/3Uw7FbT (2020).

Cambridge Elements ☰

Sustainability: Science, Policy, Practice

About the Series
This series showcases scholarship that investigates persistent, multi-scale challenges to global sustainability. It facilitates the consolidation of the science and social science of sustainability, bridging the gap between knowledge, policy, and practice. It aims to include the best reviews of relevant themes related to environment, development, and sustainability.

Cambridge Elements ≡

Sustainability: Science, Policy, Practice

Elements in the Series

A full series listing is available at: www.cambridge.org/ESBL